IMPRESSIONS OF INDIA

IMPRESSIONS OF INDIA

SIR HENRY CRAIK, K.C.B., M. P.

GYAN

Published by

GYAN

Gyan Publishing House
5, Ansari Road
Daryaganj, New Delhi-110002
Phone: 011-47034999, 9811692060
E-mail: books@gyanbooks.com

Distribution Network
gyanbooks.com
India, USA, Canada, UK, Australia, France

ISBN: 978-81-212-8824-8 (PB)
First Published, 1908

2nd Impression 2023

Printed at: Gyan Press, Delhi.

IMPRESSIONS OF INDIA
Author: Henry Craik

IMPRESSIONS OF INDIA

MACMILLAN AND CO., Limited
LONDON · BOMBAY · CALCUTTA
MELBOURNE

THE MACMILLAN COMPANY
NEW YORK · BOSTON · CHICAGO
ATLANTA · SAN FRANCISCO

THE MACMILLAN CO. OF CANADA, Ltd.
TORONTO

IMPRESSIONS OF INDIA

BY

Sir HENRY CRAIK, K.C.B., M.P.

MACMILLAN AND CO., LIMITED
ST. MARTIN'S STREET, LONDON
1908

PREFACE

THESE impressions of a tour through India, made during the winter of 1907-8, are presented in no spirit of dogmatism. They are simply the record of personal observation, aided by abundant conferences with those who had the best right to pronounce an authoritative judgment, whether amongst the native races or amongst our own countrymen. I have sought to avoid the presumption of pronouncing judgment upon problems on which long experience alone entitles one to have definite opinions, as well as the danger of saying one word which might increase the difficulties of those responsible for Indian administration.

The notes appeared originally in the columns of the *Scotsman*, and are reprinted only at the suggestion of those, both here and in India, to whom they seemed to have some little interest. Those who command ripest experience sometimes, from their very familiarity, forget, and are therefore unable to describe, the contrasts that have most piquancy and freshness for the reader at home.

H. C.

CONTENTS

I

ON THE WAY

S.S. "MACEDONIA," ARABIAN SEA,
October 24, 1907.

WELL-NIGH one thousand souls, thrown together from all countries and peoples for a solid three weeks—confined within a space of some 400 feet in length by 40 feet in breadth! We shall be separated in some twelve hours, and these weeks that have bulked so largely, that have seemed so interminable, will be only a memory. Sum together all the planning, all the devisings, all the absorption in their own purposes of each and all of these thousand souls; think of the labour and the time that they involved—and to-morrow we shall no longer be the entity we have been for three weeks, the living contents of a great ship, sharing its lot, watching its progress, criticising its conduct, paying it the respect due to the dominating influence, for the time being, in the lives of us all—a respect that may, and does, vary from violent aversion to warm affection, but which has at least the element of reverence, commanded by unquestionable superiority of power. It is an odd conjunction, like to nothing else in human experience—that of a ship's-load of beings, to whom, for the nonce, the sharing of a common life has the force of a welding power. We have been cherishing, no doubt, each our own opinion, on ourselves, on the ship, on her crew, on the weather, on the voyage, on all the experiences we have shared; but in spite of our variety we have been for three weeks an integral whole in the mass of humanity, unable to break away, mentally or morally, from its thraldom. To-morrow we shall be scattered like chaff, and we shall have to make an effort to recall the experiences of the voyage.

One thing will be quite ineffaceable in that memory, and that is that we have been an uncommonly large company. We have the highest respect for one another; but in one opinion we all agree—that a good many of us might be absent without loss to the general comfort. A ship is not run as a benevolent effort, and shareholders naturally look for dividends. It would not tend to produce dividends if ships sailed without their due complement. Ours is well provided, and we are, no doubt, ill to please if we do not find her spacious. But there are limits to human powers, and especially to the social faculties; and three weeks are not long enough for the most large-hearted to find room for four hundred new friends. To put it plainly, we are still shy of one another. We have sampled one another; we have studied our fellow-passengers as one studies the contents of a Royal Academy. As for knowing them, we are much where we were three weeks ago. How quickly we become conventional! We have our stock jokes and our stock grievances; our stock remarks on the weather and on the incidents of the voyage; our stock judgments; and our stock likes and dislikes. And they lie almost as much on the surface as if we were members of the same little social nucleus at home. The notions of what is or is not proper and permissible have become highly developed; and I am convinced that if we came to analyse the genesis of the social code that now guides us, we would find that we have developed many very distinct opinions which were not present in our minds, even in embryo, three weeks ago. Our faculty of evolving new phases of Mrs. Grundyism is truly marvellous.

We have our common grievances, and we have found that common afflictions have a wonderful effect in welding sympathies. The patience of humanity has never been more miraculously exhibited than in its suffering of the exquisite torture that is caused to the unoffending traveller by that worst form of noxious animal, the common or ordinary ship-infesting child. Unlike other pests of the same kind, this creature is the product, not of nature, but of highly-developed artificial craft. Judging from many specimens on board, the natural product is not only not offensive, but may be particularly charming. But it is clearly an ambition cultivated with assiduity by certain parents that their children should be carefully trained to inflict the maximum of torture with the most subtle ingenuity upon all the unfortunates in their neighbourhood. And yet (let it be said to the credit of the patience, if not of the self-assertion, of humanity), this torture is endured with scarcely a murmur; and the mothers—dear creatures—continue to be enraptured with the attention paid to those highly-developed instruments of torture for which they are responsible, and which they have spared no pains to foster into their present eminence of obnoxiousness. One is forced sometimes to wonder whether we are not miracles of moral cowardice, rather than examples of long-suffering patience. When will a steamship company have the fortitude and the commercial foresight to close certain ships to the presence of these joys of humanity? Those who would miss their presence might be permitted to cast in their lot with them, and leave others who cultivate a quiet life to cross the sea amidst something else than the eternal *infantum vagitus.*

Well, it is nearing its end now—this little life within life; and as it hastens to its close, one is disposed to take stock of the use we have made of it. Look back only a few years, and think what any man would have learned in passing over these few thousand miles—how crowded would have been his experiences, how much would have been added to his life, how changed a man he would have been! We have hurried through all the scenes that have framed the history, the poetry, the romance of the world—and what the better are we? Our most remarkable adventures have been with boatmen and railway porters. Our severest trials have been to wait for our turn at the morning bath. Our most serious thoughts have had to be devoted to the selection from amongst the multitudinous contents of an overladen menu. The most active form of exertion has been the playing of deck quoits—not exactly an adventurous form of sport—and Homeric contests of lady cricketers with a men's team compelled to keep their right hands in their pockets. Verily we who are globe-trotters are a feeble folk. We have been coddled into very miracles of flaccid imbecility. One thing only is left us as a sort of salve to the conscience that slumbers in its luxurious inutility: we may watch humbly and strive to learn a little from those fellow-travellers who are sharing our lotus-eating and our cushioned ease for the nonce, but who have to take up a different rôle when they reach the journey's end—those who must face the enigma of the East, and keep their touch on the pulse of Empire. The last thing they are thinking about now is giving us much-needed instruction, of dividing themselves off from the luxurious and useless crowd of drones amongst whom their lot is meantime cast.

Only occasionally, when confidences are to some extent exchanged, are we allowed to see the mingled anger and contempt that may be engendered by certain vapid mouthings of ignorance and self-conceit. But the mountebankism of the political charlatan is accepted rather with the contempt of neglect than with any ferocity of indignation. As we mark it, our dominant feeling is not precisely that of profound pride in our British House of Commons as it has most recently been represented in India, nor that of unbounded confidence in the respect and affection that have been won for it by recent escapades there.

II

IN BOMBAY

LAHORE, *October* 30, 1907.

AT last, on Friday the 25th October, we were at Bombay. As if under the guise of being loath to part with us, the ship went leisurely for the last day; and as the end of our time on board was near, we no doubt felt a twinge of regret at saying good-bye. The last night was a restless and disturbed one; no one could settle to sleep; the ship-load was awake and stirring at an unearthly hour. The burden of packing up lay heavy on the minds of the ladies; and there was only a pretence of slumber before we dropped anchor in front of the long front of Bombay, gleaming bright in the hazy dawn of a perfect morning. To most of those on board it is as familiar as Southampton Water; to all, the sea view of

Bombay seems a subject so hackneyed as to make any new attempt at description quite inept. But, after all, it is the first aspect of India, and to those to whom all the mysterious life behind is a new and untried thing it is full of meaning. He would be over-bold who attempted description of such a scene; but even the novice sees something which is veiled from the familiar eye. All who have had years of correspondence with India can tell the same story—how it is the earlier letters that give us the descriptive touches; how their vividness gradually diminishes and then fades away; and how in the end discussion of political questions, and careful judgments on Indian social and economical problems, come to take the place of description, and we are fain to do without those pictures of everyday life that gradually withdraw themselves from the observation of those to whom they are things of every day.

Our landing is no simple and unadventurous episode. As if to mark our arrival in a new country, the P. and O. Company introduces us to some breakneck experiences in the descent from the ship to the tender. There are mysterious and sufficient reasons for it, no doubt, and we must take what comes with a trusting faith that nothing better can be devised. But the thought will obtrude that the splendid organisation of our ship might have contrived something better than the perils of an Alpine descent, without ropes and guides, for their departing guests. However, all's well that ends well, and we are safely landed without mishap.

One thing strikes the male mind, with its limited faculty of contrivance, in that landing: it is the genius of our Anglo-Indian sisters for getting rid of any appearance of the dishevelment and untidiness that travel generally produces. It was marvellous how, after a disturbed and broken night, after three weeks of living in close quarters, amid all the noise and bustle of an eager crowd, and with a disembarkation in the early hours of the morning, there was not one who might not have walked straight from the ship to a garden party. It was in striking contrast with the landing at Dover of any company of English travellers after the Channel passage.

Then all attention to appearance is neglected, and our ladies scramble on shore in happy faith that the miseries of others will afford security against any scanning of toilettes. Their achievements at Bombay prove convincingly that when put to the test they are amply capable of better things. We landed —as we were led to understand—no fewer than seventeen prospective brides, and all of them stepped on shore so well groomed that they need not have feared to go straight to the altar. The fatigues of packing, the bustle of gathering luggage, the hurry and scurry of the endless troubles of disembarkation, had left not the slightest traces on their equipment. I must leave it to the more contriving sex to explain the problem.

What are our first impressions? First, as we pass through the streets, the countless legions of dark-hued faces, the strange rarity of the white complexion. It is not that we are outnumbered. To all intents and purposes, so far as numbers go, we simply do not count. And next, amongst these countless dark visages, the endless variety of physiognomy, with only one common attribute, that of absolute inscrutability. They are solemn and self-important, or careless and self-forgetful; they are dreamy and ferocious, melancholy and merry; but all alike are to us simply masks. They look at us as if they were divided from us by centuries, and as if they were gazing at sticks and stones. Their lives lie hidden away from us by an impenetrable veil. In London we hear glib talk of the need of greater sympathy with the native. What easy words to utter!

Next, the quietness, the coolness, the patience, the reserve of authority, of the few white faces that we meet. No wonder that with men like these, who know their work, its hard conditions and its dangers, and have learned to face it, the recklessness of loose tongues is met by a momentary anger perhaps, but, after the first moment, with the apathy of contempt. There is something of strain, and no great measure of light-heartedness, in the faces of that ruling class; but no fretfulness and nervousness, and no assumption of bullying or domineering. They are there to do their duty; and almost the only comment, if we refer to the wild mouthings of self-advertising frivolity, is, "Why heed him?"

Of the general appearance of Bombay I am conscious that it requires some temerity for a new-comer to speak. One thing adds infinitely to its picturesqueness, as compared with a South African town: there is no banning from the streets of native costume, or even lack of costume, and this, as it seems to me, is all to the good. The ugliest sight one can see in Durban or Johannesburg is the native clad in European dress; the most attractive sight in the thoroughfares of Bombay is the native in his many-coloured garb, and with that lissomeness of limb which its freedom gives. All along the Queen's Road, the promenade which runs along the sea to Malabar Hill, crowded as it is with carriages, motors, and bullock-carts, we come across natives peacefully sleeping on the side paths, or quietly cooking their meals in the airiest of garments. We pass the fishing village, and then climb the road to Malabar Hill, and on between picturesque gardens and the many-coloured villas of the wealthier natives, with their bright tiles glittering in the sun. It is a picture which we could see nowhere else, and even the stifling heat is relieved by the breeze which comes from the wide expanse of sea on each side of us.

Of Bombay as a city, what can one say? Its sea-front looks bright and magnificent from the harbour—what large piles of sumptuous buildings could look otherwise in such a sunlight? The great mass of the Taj Hotel dominates them all. It shows itself frankly for what it is—a huge advertisement, brave in its rather exaggerated caricature of an Indian palace. The great ranges of flats and mansions have a sumptuousness of their own, and would find themselves quite at home along the sea-front of Brighton, which they would fitly embellish. The Yacht Club is more quiet and dignified, and tells of comfort without gaudiness in its trim lawns and white balustrade. The principal commercial street would be a splendid thoroughfare in any European capital, and its warehouses, its banks, its insurance offices, need not fear comparison with the best of their kind at home. It is a thoroughfare of generous width, bordered with rows of trees, and broken here and there by public gardens rich with flowers. Bombay there displays its wealth, but for real interest we must go to the narrow and crowded streets of the native town, down the passage of the Bazaar, where natives of every tribe are chattering and gesticulating, while at every second or third stall the vendor is peacefully sleeping after his morning's work, and crowds of infants grin at us merrily from the corners and the recesses at the back. Occasionally a specially active stall-holder offers us his wares; for the most part they only turn on us a vacant and preoccupied glance, and sink back into their own inscrutable indifference.

It is a brilliant city, brimful of interest in its native quarter, lavish in its display of wealth in the business streets, picturesque in its residential suburbs, with their wealth of colour and of foliage. It may be a heresy, but to my mind there is one, and only one, British building of real architectural beauty in Bombay. It is the old Town Hall, built, I suppose, in the eighteenth century, when the Adam influence was strong, and when our great-grandfathers struck what one is tempted to think was the true note—that of making their buildings distinctive of our national character, and attempting no flimsy imitations in the Indo-Saracenic style. Those who, no doubt, know better will condemn my bad taste; but, frankly, I must confess that this fashion of aping the beauties of an alien style does not attract me. The University does not carry this too far, and has an architectural beauty of its own. The Secretariat might have been even more imposing with advantage, as the outward embodiment of our rule. But the railway stations, with their extravagant decoration, their air of exaggerated splendour, and, above all, their inharmonious imitation of the Eastern style, strike one only as inept and misplaced. One wonders what the educated native must think of these caricatures of Indian palaces, built at lavish expense, to house the noise and bustle and confusion and discomfort of an Indian terminus. No stranger can be confident in criticism; but the thought inevitably obtrudes itself whether some of the millions of rupees spent upon the Victoria terminus might not have been better applied to increase the comforts of the traveller on the G.I.P. Railway.

Because the traveller must be warned that he has not overcome the troubles of a trip to India when he has completed the 6000 miles of the outward voyage, with all its elaborate organisation and contrivances for comfort. He has still to face the railway journey on the G.I.P., and his experience there will not soon be forgotten. Crowded and ill-constructed carriages, the absence of corridors, inattentive and indifferent attendants, and a total lack of all the amenities which elsewhere have made us perhaps too fastidious—these make the 1300 miles to Lahore a dolorous and toilsome journey. Government railway management has no doubt its own advantages; but an experience of the G.I.P. makes it not surprising that Indian travellers view with misgiving the future extension of Government control, and gives those of us who come from home reason to doubt its advantages if applied there. But, at least, a Government railway should have a fair start in modern rolling-stock. In this respect the G.I.P. is thirty years behind Rhodesia, and twenty years behind the Sudan. Nor are its hardships compensated by any large measure of security. I have been six days in India, and in that time there have been three serious accidents between Bombay and Lahore. My experience may, no doubt, have been unfortunate, and one must not generalise too quickly. I shall live in hope of better things elsewhere in India.

Forty-two hours of railway travelling, with such scant appliances, and with trying extremes of heat and cold, make one glad to glide at last into the ease and quiet of the residential quarter at Lahore. I had heard much of its plague of dust; I can only say that I have been able to bear with equanimity elsewhere much more overpowering visitations of that kind than I have yet experienced at Lahore, even after an abnormally dry season. In its quiet vistas of green foliage, in its cool and shady gardens, in its long avenues of rides and drives, one finds a perfect centre to gain a passing and perhaps only a superficial view of the realities of Indian life.

III

LAHORE, PAST AND PRESENT

LAHORE, *November* 7, 1907.

EVEN absolute ignorance may be forgiven if it aspires to do no more than record impressions; and a week in Lahore gives these in a very distinct shape. In the first place, coming straight here from Bombay, one soon feels the presence of the distinctive type of the Sikh. There is far less of the *dolce far niente* life that one notes along the Queen's Road and on the shady lanes of Malabar Hill. You see, in the opening days of the cooler weather which never visits Bombay, fewer of the sparsely clothed and sinewy limbs, far less of the gay colouring, than is in evidence in the sunshine and brilliance of the southern city. But once seen, the Sikh is not unnoticed or easily forgotten. He is the very type of a fighting race. With their stalwart figures, the chakras or war-quoits twisted in their puggarees, their long uncut hair and beard, and the stateliness of their gait, his fellow-tribesmen soon make themselves distinctive. The other day, during our morning ride, we passed a regiment—the 14th Sikhs—in marching order, on their way from Ferozepore, through Lahore, to the frontier, and a finer lot of men it has never been my lot to see — even in the Egyptian or Sudanese regiments, and for physique these are hard to beat. At their head marched the priests of the regiment, in pure white muslin robes. Their uniform was admirably serviceable, and at the same time strikingly picturesque: long blue tunics, loosely made; khaki-coloured trousers; white puggarees, each with the war-quoit twisted in its folds. Without exception they were much above middle height, and their sergeants, as the elders of the corps, were models of dignity with their long grey beards. They kept perfect rank, and stepped out in perfect time, but at the same time with an easy long swing that it would be hard for any European regiment to rival. A long train of light mule-carts carried their baggage, and they passed along with no rattling of chains, no jolting of heavy wheels, no creaking of clumsy waggons. Even on the roads, which all about Lahore now are suffering from protracted drought, they raised surprisingly little dust.

The Sikh is the most characteristic type here; but it was not he who constructed the fast-crumbling monuments which were once the glory of Lahore. It has a history old enough — going far back beyond any trustworthy annals. When Alexander the Great was here, Lahore—although even its name in those ages is doubtful—was certainly an imposing city. There are temples and mosques, and tombs by the score, although some of them have crumbled into such decay that the very remnants of their former brilliance are gone, and many are scarcely distinguishable from tumble-down and deserted houses. But all these are of later date than the era of Hindu rule, and it is their destruction, not their construction, that is to be credited to the Sikh. He was essentially a man of war, not an artist or a builder.

The epoch of splendour for Lahore was the seventeenth century—when the Great Mogul was the embodiment of almost fabulous sway and boundless wealth—amidst the glories of Shah Jahan's rule, when he held the throne at Delhi, and his Vizier, Wazir Khan, administered Lahore. Akbar, Jahingar, Shah Jahan, and Aurungzeb, each had a greatness of his own, and the names of all live in the monuments of Lahore to-day. One can imagine the impression that the magnificence of their rule made upon our own travellers of that day—Coryat, Sir Thomas Herbert, Sir Thomas Roe, and Hawkins. No wonder that they wrote rapturously of the wealth of India, and dwelt on the magnificence of the Great Mogul, and that Milton goes "to Agra and Lahore of Great Mogul" for the type of barbaric splendour.

Imagine a city standing on a space of less than five hundred acres, inhabited by a teeming population, pent up in narrow, twisted streets, and girt by a wall with thirteen gates. Within its narrow limits, palaces and gardens, spacious and splendid mosques, with towering minarets and gilded domes, wedged in by narrow streets of shops and rabbit warrens of houses, all decorated with marvellous lattice-work carved in teak, and bright with hangings of every hue. The walls of the city still stand; the crowded buildings still in many cases retain their dainty lattice-work, all dusty and decayed. The bright hangings are almost gone, and instead the streets are often overhung by heavy curtains to keep out the sun, pitched so low that they had many times to be removed to allow our elephant to pass. For a good view of the city there is no vehicle so convenient as the howdah of the Lieutenant-Governor's elephant, which was graciously lent us for the journey—a journey which the narrowness of the crowded streets would make impossible for a carriage, and which would have its discomfort for a foot passenger. Some of the mosques still glitter with their gilded minarets, and sparkle in the sun with the wondrous beauty of their tiles. The narrow streets still house the greater part of a population of some 200,000 souls. The same varied types of face, each striking in its way, still peer from behind their booths, and business still has its perpetual hum and bustle. We get glimpses into interiors overhead that might be reflected from an age of fabulous story and romance. But all the splendour and the gorgeousness have gone. All the pomp and all the relentless cruelty, all the luxury and all the degradation, are gone as a light that has vanished, and in their place to outward seeming there is nothing but crumbling and squalor and decay. Only we know that behind some of these walls there are housed men of ancient race, of names that have their place in history, and others who have amassed, by modern methods, stores of wealth that would enable them to buy out all those who spend their lives and their strength in governing this vast community, of which they form only an infinitesimal proportion—say 1 or 2 per cent. Without their controlling hand, how soon the pent-up jealousies of race and religion would burst all restraining bounds?

Beyond these walls, when the Great Mogul reigned and before the Sikh had worked his will on those splendid monuments, for which he had no taste, there spread for miles a long succession of great houses and splendid gardens, interspersed with tombs of costly workmanship. Almost all of them have passed away, or left but shadows of themselves. Here and there a tomb attracts us, by fragments of fair tilework and delicate carving—which time would have spared had the hand of the destroyer been absent, and which owe such preservation as now retains some of their beauty to the care of Lahore's present rulers. Above all, there is "The House of Joy"—the Shalimar Garden—still spreading in leafy beauty, and with a wealth of cunning marble-work, under a heavy coating of dust—with its canals and ponds all dry and empty, and its sparkling fountains silent,—a fitting monument of exhausted luxury, where even Ranjit Singh still held high revels some seventy years gone by, although his hands stript it of many of its costly decorations. The other gardens and spacious palaces have crumbled to the dust, and in their place there are the broad avenues of the English residential quarter, with its pleasant compounds and bungalows, interspersed with some mansions of the native aristocracy. It is in that broad space that we find the handsome edifices reared by the modern rulers: the Chief Court, Government House, Montgomery and Lawrence Halls, the Hospitals, University College, the English and Roman Catholic Cathedrals, the Museum, the Aitchison College for the Rajahs' sons, and numerous schools. They tell of another aspect of affairs, in which lavish magnificence, the splendour of lost arts, the pride of despotism, have given place to quiet work, to unresting effort in a stupendous task, to the simplicity of a self-restrained life, to even-handed justice. That is Lahore to-day.

IV

LAHORE: ITS CRIMINAL, EDUCATIONAL, & RELIGIOUS SIGHTS

RAWAL PINDI, *November* 10, 1907.

FIRST impressions do not give you the whole of Lahore; but a larger acquaintance enlarges rather than changes them. This week the town has been making holiday for the close of Ramadan, and yesterday it was *en fête*, and the brilliantly coloured dresses gave it a new aspect of brightness and of gaiety. It was *Id*—that, I think, is the conventional way of representing the word in our characters, although phonetically I would have been inclined to spell it *Eed*—or the new moon which ends the fast; and in the great mosque of Akbar there was a vast gathering to greet its appearance—which must be duly announced by two witnesses of authority—with one simultaneous bow of devotion and the intoned call of Allah pu Akbar—God is greatest. Lahore proved that it could readily change its usual monotone of colour for brighter garb, and all—adults and children alike—were decked in all the hues of the rainbow. Amid vague rumours of unrest it was no bad sight to watch the crowds passing in file across the steps of the Queen Victoria Memorial—which has been recently covered in by a marble canopy of delicate tracery—and paying their reverential salaams to the White Mother and the embodiment of even-handed justice. If there was disloyalty amongst these crowds of Zemindars that gathered into the city from the country round, it certainly managed to conceal itself very satisfactorily. The week gave a new aspect to the place. But there is more to be learned in Lahore which does not show on the surface. You see at first only the strenuous lives of the British community, the evidence meeting you at every turn that there is no room here for the loafer or the idler. No one is here merely to please himself. You may criticise their methods—I find it difficult to do so—but you cannot deny their energy. The Montgomery Institute and its gardens are gay enough in the late afternoon, and one might think for a moment that the crowds that gather there live for tennis or Badminton. But drive through the gardens at 4.30, and you will find them a desert. Ten minutes later they are full; and at six o'clock darkness falls all of a sudden, and the coolies are rolling away the tennis nets and screens. The rest of the day is filled with work. Of that you may learn a good deal even from casual talk. One official will tell you of the strange devices of the Pathans in search of firearms, which it is his business to detect. They have to be tracked across the jungle; and in little groups of five or six, meeting at some distant point during the night, and by day wandering singly about the towns disguised as pedlars, they pass far south of Lahore after this one quest—the impounding of guns, which fetch about £100 apiece in their own country. Their boldness is marvellous. They have been known to enter an

English barracks in the quiet of the early afternoon, when Tommy Atkins is resting after dinner, and to carry out a stand of arms without detection. Once obtained, the guns are broken up and disposed in pieces about their clothes or buried in a convenient spot. Their devices for conveying them across the border are endless. A doleful procession came to a railway station with the coffin of their deceased relative. Their piety compelled them to bury him in the country of his birth, and this they did in spite of obvious signs that their business was unsavoury and insanitary. Native prejudices must be respected, and the railway officials naturally gave them a wide berth, and a truck for their exclusive use—glad to be rid of their malodorous burden. At last a police officer suspected motives other than those of filial piety, and braving the obstacles that made further investigation difficult, required them to submit the coffin for inspection. The little company of bereaved relatives fled *instanter*, leaving the officer to find on searching the coffin a goodly store of purloined rifles and—a dead dog! So keen and relentless is their pursuit of guns, that officers have been compelled to have pits dug for storing ammunition by night and to make soldiers sleep over these temporary storehouses. To guard against such thieves as these is only one branch of the policeman's work. There are whole tribes—officially recognised as Criminal Tribes—whose avowed and only calling is theft, and against whose depredations town and country have alike to be protected. Add the endless ramifications of tribe feuds and their consequences in crimes of violence; the unresting vigilance of the train-thief and the house-breaker, the constant occurrence of dacoity, and, above all, the utter hopelessness of procuring any evidence worth the name—and we may well believe that the policeman's lot in the Punjab is "not a happy one." And we must remember that the English supervisor has to spend no small part of his vigilant care in guarding against the inclination of his native subordinate to that high-handed tyranny which, in the view of the East, is the natural concomitant of all authority. It does not take one long to see that the readiest oppressor of the native is the native subordinate official.

Another side of criminal administration at Lahore is the prison—which is the central prison of the Punjab for long sentence prisoners. Something it has of the usual aspect of such establishments—their orderliness, their perfection of cleanliness, their silence. But it stands out with a pre-eminence of its own. It is the most healthy, the airiest, the cleanest, the most restful spot in Lahore. Its grounds are spacious and well cultivated, with enough of trees to break the flood of sunshine. That sunshine banishes the prevailing gloom of an English prison, and its rays are no trial, but unmixed gain, to most of the inmates. Save for the one boon of liberty, it is hard to say in what respect the lot of the prisoners whom we saw was not a happier one than that of their poorer brethren beyond the prison gates. About the prisoners two or three things were noticeable: first, the vastly preponderating proportion of habitual prisoners; next, the number of those who came, not from the crowded cities, but from the remote country districts—impelled to crime by racial, local, or family feuds; lastly, the number of very old men, and those whom we would count as almost children, condemned for murder or some crime of violence. As for the old men, one is inclined to believe that some of them were suffering vicariously. They had no vicious faces, and were often too old and weak to hurt any living thing. But they were there by their own confession and by the sworn evidence of their own kin. It is to be feared that family interest and selfishness may sometimes prompt the sacrifice of an old man past work in place of a younger and stronger malefactor. Of the younger prisoners, it was easy to predict that their only safe habitation for life was the jail. They had faces, for the most part, typically criminal beyond all hope of recall. One young villain of twelve was pointed out as a murderer, and I would rather not be alone with him if he were free and had a knife ready to hand. Yet the effort to reclaim is not abandoned. They were under gymnastic instruction when we were there, and did credit to their instructor; they knew something of geography and of contemporary history; and the present Secretary of State for India would have been amused to hear the alacrity with which his portrait was recognised and greeted by these youthful and precocious ruffians. They are kindly treated, but the less they get beyond that treatment for the remainder of their lives the better it will be for those outside.

A notably contrasted sphere of work is that to be seen at the Aitchison College for the young chiefs. I do not presume to give any educational estimate of its work. That would be outside of my present aim, which is to give only the picture presented to the casual traveller. I have no doubt whatever that the expenditure is wise and politic, and of the efficiency of the management I am thoroughly convinced. But let us look only at the salient features of the institution. We enter a spacious, well-timbered park, where, at wide and convenient distances, stately buildings rise. There are chapels, class-rooms, living-rooms, dining-rooms, gymnasia, stables —all on an imposing scale. Long avenues of trees and spacious playing fields spread on every side. In England the dimensions would seem abundant in space for a high-class school of 500 or 600 boys. Here there are some 80 pupils in attendance. The class-rooms are lofty and dignified apartments, like the reading-rooms of a well-equipped club. The dining-rooms are imposing, and round the tables are ranged *arm-chairs* for the students as they dine. The living-rooms are copiously furnished, and for the most part they comprise sitting-room as well as bed-room. An Eton or Harrow boy would look askance at the luxury; and, compared with it, Long Chamber at Eton is as a hovel to a palace. Even a wealthy chief estimated the cost on account of his two sons at about £200 a year; and many of the chiefs whose wealth does not keep measure with their family influence are allowed to send their sons there at little more than a nominal fee. We talked with some of the young chiefs, whose ages range from 8 to 17. They represented every tribe, and various races and religions. Their dress varied from costly silk with gold em-broidery to more sombre hues. Amongst them all there was not a face which did not compel a lingering examination, and many were strikingly handsome. One unaccustomed to judge of Eastern development would have put the age of the older boys at two or three and twenty rather than seventeen. Most of them spoke English with facility, and all had the manners and the deportment of the aristocrat. It is a scheme conceived by a bold imagination, sumptuously full of high promise. Its outer aspect is all that I attempt to give. Let me add that one boy was pointed out to me who could not return home for his holidays because his life would not have been safe from those who are hostile to his succession. It is an epitome of our rule in India.

Another day was spent at Amritsar, the centre of the Sikh religion, where the central feature is the Golden Temple, built in the middle of a great tank, and raised with the extravagant lavishness of costly luxury, rather than in the spirit of high art, by Ranjit Singh less than a hundred years ago. Its decorations were in large measure obtained by the indiscriminate plunder of other buildings erected elsewhere under a more artistic impulse. But its very splendour is imposing, and more especially so when it is occupied, as it was when we saw it, by a vast concourse of various races and religions—including Mussulmans—who found in the Fair of the Dewali an opportunity for indulging in their favourite pastime of a religious pilgrimage even though they could not share in its religious rites. We were conducted to the central shrine, where the Sikh Scripture reposed upon a mass of cushions, where the crowds pressed round to present their offerings and receive the accustomed blessing, and where pigeons, alighting close to the pile of cushions, calmly cropped the grain and spice that lay heaped upon the floor; while a band discoursed music and chanted a hymn that had perhaps more of the voluptuous than the devotional in its rhythm. There was no resentment at the intrusion of European visitors. Our conductor, a high medical official, was on the best terms with all, and chatted familiarly with the warrior priests who stood about in a strange panoply of ancient weapons of war. Everywhere we met with ready and kindly courtesy. For our behoof the ceremony of the Sikh baptism was enacted on two young neophytes. The catechism was duly recited and answered;

the vows were taken, including the vow of loyalty to the Emperor of India; the neophytes were sprinkled with water, and helped one another to the sacred food in token of brothership, and then passed to join the crowds who were bathing in the huge sacred tank. Within the enclosure we were a tiny company of Europeans in a vast dusky crowd; yet there was not a single failure in the courtesy with which way was readily made for us. A native sense of dignity prevented any hustling or undue curiosity; and the apathy of the East was shown by the figures which lay wrapped in quiet sleep upon the marble pavement amid the surging crowd. A somewhat jarring note was struck by the gewgaws of the temporary decorations (!), which would have been better in their place on the outskirts of a booth at a provincial fair; but it was not unsatisfactory to see that one of them bore an inscription of "Welcome" to the Deputy Commissioner. There appeared to be a slump in "unrest" and disloyalty.

We had yet to visit the Fort at Lahore, where a small English garrison is housed, high above the native city and amidst the remains of the Mogul Palace, now being restored by the care of the British Government, and retaining even in its decay traces of its former beauty. Its use as an object-lesson to what might be turbulent forces is perhaps more morally than physically effective, but it serves its purpose, and could not, I fancy, safely be abandoned without some very efficient substitute, so long as the mass of our military force lies some four miles off at Mianmir. It lay beside the vast mosque of Akbar, and the view of the old city from its heights is singularly picturesque. There is one more of the sights of Lahore not to be omitted—the Shahdara or mausoleum erected by Shah Jahan to his father, Jahangir, which lies some four miles to the north beyond the river Ravi. Quite recently the vast garden round it has been cleared of overcrowded trees, and the beauty of the monument is better visible. It is in the most perfect style of that art which the Mogul encouraged, but which he seems to have executed not through native genius, but by the employment of Italian artists. The trace of Italian design is present at every turn, and it is strange to think that so much of what we are apt to regard as monuments of Eastern resourcefulness was really the work of artists of the West attracted by the Mogul's wealth. All the money that can be spared is now wisely spent in restoring some of the former grace of monuments like this, and the Shahdara will soon be again—if, indeed, it is not now—one of the most perfect of those works of penetrating beauty which rest in the memory. Its vast square, rich in colour, its four lofty minarets, bright with inlaid stone and glittering with marble balustrades, its spacious and spreading lawns, form, perhaps, of all the sights of Lahore that which is its chief gem. One thinks with wonder how the Eastern mind must view the careful preservation and the deft restoration by the hand of their present rulers of these monuments of their ancient cult! It is a secret hidden in their breasts.

For a time I have left Lahore, for a visit to the Frontier Province.

V

IN THE NORTH-WEST: HINDU INTRIGUE

IN CAMP AT BALABGAHR,
NEAR DELHI, *November* 20.

THE move northwards to Rawal Pindi from Lahore means another venture on what may be a trying ordeal—a journey on an Indian railway. So far—with all possible desire to avoid reckless criticism—I am bound to say that my experience has not been good. The responsible management is no doubt excellent; but letters which would receive a reply by return of post from any railway company at home, get into the hands of some native or Eurasian sub-official, and you are lucky if you get an answer in a week. At the stations the comfort of passengers is a negligible quantity. A train may start at its advertised time; but if some mails do not happen to have arrived, it is not impossible that it may wait for two or three hours, and dawdle along the journey, so that you arrive at your destination some four hours after time, in a six hours' run. High officials may be treated with a consideration denied to the ordinary traveller; if not, they must have a store of patience which is beyond praise. The native fares immeasurably worse. Government may issue edifying ukases on the considerate treatment of the native, but such exhortations have something of an air of hypocrisy when one sees how native third-class passengers are treated on Government lines. I may be told that the native likes to be crowded and jostled. I shall believe as soon that the eels like to be skinned. Frankly, I have seen scenes in crowded trains in India of which I think it would be well that the Government should be spared the discredit. I speak now in the interests of the native, not of the European traveller.

But even an Indian railway journey must have an end, and we are now approaching Rawal Pindi, and are rising into the hills. It is an extraordinary country through which we are passing. It is nothing but a series of gigantic sandhills, now dry and parched, but broken by rainstorms into a myriad of ravines, and crumbling into fragments in every direction. There are few signs of habitations, and nothing which, to the ordinary eye, seems likely to afford sustenance to a living creature, and one wonders where the scanty flocks of goats obtain a livelihood. Dry nullahs twist and intertwine on every side, and a more difficult or uninviting country to any advancing host it is difficult to conceive. Presently the rocks seem to become more solid; we pass through a few short tunnels, and emerge into more level country, parched and dry indeed, but with something of occasional greenness, and levelled into a plain that affords more extended views. Such is the approach to Rawal Pindi. We have left the Sikh behind, and are now amongst a more varied type. The Pathan blood is apparent, and every now and then the eye is arrested by the mountain breed.

Rawal Pindi is quiet enough now, but it has just passed through a rough experience, when the wisest and the least nervous scented danger in the air. Sedition had laid its train carefully. The best of the natives, rightly or wrongly, detected ominous signs, and were not backward to indicate them to the authorities. The danger was met by promptness and bold initiative. The native regiments remained firm, and were publicly thanked for doing so. One cannot but wonder whether to men of military instinct, as these are, thanks for performing their obvious duty could be altogether palatable. However that may be, the nerves of the wardens of Empire at Rawal Pindi are not of a sort to be easily shaken. The machine of Government works smoothly now, but intrigues and seditious plots that aim at shaking the loyalty of the Army are a sort of fuel that is dangerous near the powder magazine of the fierce passions of a Pathan population. The danger is not less when the dexterity of Hindu intrigue is aiming at stirring up the fanaticism of the Mussulmans, who are in dominant proportion here. We have here left the Sikh and the Hindu behind, and are surrounded by Mohammedans; but it does not follow that Hindu intrigue is slumbering here, and it has been helped by the scourge of the plague, and may be helped by it again. That the danger was, a few months ago, real and imminent, no one competent to form an opinion doubts. Without presuming to criticise subsequent judicial proceedings, one may regret that they have had an appearance of condoning sedition, and we can only hope that prompt and firm initiative has taught a sufficiently impressive lesson.

Rawal Pindi now lies under the same scourge of prevailing dust as Lahore — the consequence of the long drought. It has the same well-planted avenues, the same shady compounds with their well-tended lawns, with perhaps something more of brightness and of colour. The native city is far smaller in proportion than that at Lahore. There are no notable buildings of another age. The military lines are far more in evidence than those of Mianmir, which are at some distance from Lahore, and they bear a far greater proportion to the civil element. Seen as we see it now, even with all its abnormal dose of dust, Rawal Pindi is a goodly place of residence, and its surroundings have an interest of their own, as the battlefields of all the races and of all the centuries. We realise more vividly the military genius of Alexander as the memorials of his wondrous advance into these plains are seen. To have penetrated the vast tracts and mountainous ranges beyond us, and swooped down amongst countless fighting hordes, with no superiority in weapons of precision, and with the aid of strategy and discipline alone, is an achievement at which a later age may vainly wonder. All around he has left traces of his presence. His coins abound, and are constantly turned up by the plough. Copies of his bust in clay have been dug up in the fields. It is a strange experience to run out to Manikiala—some fourteen miles from Peshawar—with all the modernity of a motor car, and to feel yourself in one of the spots sacred to Buddha, and the scene of his sacrifices, and to gaze on the huge tope of massive masonry which tradition calls the tomb of Bucephalus. Tradition may play us false, and I believe careful investigation is inclined to give it the lie; but that only makes us accept it the more fervently as true in spirit at least, if not in the letter. All round lie battle-grounds of Greek and Persian, of Alexander and Timour, of Mogul and of Sikh. It was only in 1849 that it came under our sway, and that sway has not ended the undying ferocity of tribal and family feuds, which still have a fatal hold upon the fierce people of these regions.

From Rawal Pindi we move on to Peshawar by a train which has the rare merit of keeping to its time, but does so by giving itself an ample latitude—seven hours for about a hundred miles. Arrival late at night at Peshawar would have its inconveniences, and the authorities prefer to receive a new trainful otherwise than in the obscurity of darkness. The line passes through a country that is barren enough under the present drought, and the barrenness is all the sadder because almost every scrap of land shows signs of the wasted labour of the plough. The spurs of the Himalayas begin to push themselves nearer, and about six miles off we see the point where the Black Mountain expedition penetrated into the hills in 1888.

Our travelling companions are men who in

various ways are engaged in no business of their own, but whose work, either for a time or permanently, is the slow and grinding one, how to govern these rough tribes, and "by slow degrees subdue them to the useful and the good." Each has his interest and his energies alive; all alike have a longing for "home"; but they can tell of various aspects of the country, and generally manage as a hobby to penetrate below the surface and find out some of its physical or social secrets. Their actual life is in strange contrast to the succession of sport and pastime which those at home picture to themselves as representing Anglo-Indian careers. Their energy is good to see, and, one has little doubt, is good in its effects. It is none the less true that there is another aspect. In the eager race of a strenuous life the dead weight of retarding influences may be forgotten; and it is well, too, that the voice of experience—sometimes of sad experience—should make itself felt in leaving petty embroglios to work their own solution, and in allowing the slow processes of the Eastern nature some rest from the over-pressure of impetuous zeal. In the task that has to be accomplished energy and bold initiative count for much; patience, perhaps, counts for even more.

We pass for a large part of our journey alongside the apparently endless Grand Trunk Road, which runs direct from Calcutta to Peshawar. It preserves along all its length the same stately appearance, with its wide and liberal tracks for wheeled traffic, and for the flocks and herds and strings of camels that pass in constant succession beneath the shade of its broad avenues of trees. It impresses one more than even the railways with the steadfast pertinacity of administrative energy, and recalls more than anything else some of Napoleon's great military roads. Travellers along its endless stretches must move slowly indeed, but with less of discomfort than sometimes attends those who are carried by the Indian railways. I speak not without experience of both. At Attock we come to the junction of the Cabul and the Indus. There are broad beds for these rivers and their tributaries; but now the bridges most often pass over dry nullahs or a few feet of dwindling water.

We pass one cantonment after another, stretching with low barrack buildings at intervals over the arid tracts, and buried beneath a low-lying haze of dust, glistening in the setting sun. These form the cantonment of Nowshera. As we approach Peshawar the country becomes more green. Irrigation is there far more complete than at Rawal Pindi or even at Lahore, where the canals are only filled at intervals, and where you pass on one morning a broad and brimful canal to find a week later its waters diverted elsewhere, and in their place a channel several feet deep, and as dry as the desert. At Peshawar irrigation is constant and abundant, and to this is due its restful expanses of shady avenues, its well-watered roads, its deep recesses of bungalow compounds, with their wealth of flowers. Because, without doubt, Peshawar is the fairest town that I have yet seen in India. It stands by itself. "Peshawar," remarked a high official to me, "is not India; it is Central Asia." Here we are fairly in the Frontier Province, which has a character all its own, marked at every turn by the new aspect which our rule assumes, by the wild figures that meet us, by the self-evident proximity of the independent tribes, whose centuries of fighting have driven themselves into the fibre of their being. Hindu intrigue may work its wily way here, but were our rule absent this would be no land for the Hindu Babu. Mussulman fanaticism is only slumbering, and, once uncurbed, it would soon plunge its fangs deep into the throats of all who did not own its sway and did not draw their lineage from these independent tribes.

The life of Peshawar is strenuous. Problems hard of solution are arising there every day and every hour, to test the mettle of its administration. Its climate, so perfect now, is terrible in the warm months, and it has to dread a new visitation of the plague, which is a recent and an unwelcome intruder. It is not unnatural that those on whom the burden of what is, after all, a military outpost lies should feel the lack of sympathy for their difficulties which distance breeds. But Peshawar has its compensations, and it only proves its energy in making the best use of them in its scanty leisure. Nowhere are the roads so beautiful, in their broad and stately amplitude, closed in by distant views of the mountains, touched by ever-varying sunlight, and with the dust fiend very successfully dealt with. The golf course is a broad expanse of woodland beauty, and beyond it you reach a polo ground that claims to be the greenest and most picturesque in India, and, without claiming to make comparison, I can vouch that it is hard to beat. It lies in the circumference of the hills, and beneath the shadow of the old fort, which intervenes between it and the native city. The hunting at Peshawar, which is just beginning, claims to be at least the equal of any other in the country. It requires knowledge of the ground, and a clever pony, accustomed to negotiate "gridiron" jumps; but in the grandeur of the mountain background and the wealth of greenery, in the exhilarating crispness of the morning air, it has accompaniments that could scarcely be found elsewhere.

The city itself is full of interest, with its throng of strangely assorted crowds; but in most respects it is the very antithesis of

Lahore. There are no imposing buildings, no remnants of vast and costly mosques. Old though the city is, it has been often ravaged by fires, which easily sweep away its flimsy buildings of mud and wood, and which have allowed it to be reconstructed with streets of ample breadth. From the gate by which we entered, wide streets lead up, through a well-ordered market-place, to the eminence where the Tesil, or tax-collector's office, stands, from the roof of which you obtain a view of marvellous beauty over the roofs of the houses to the mountains in the distance, and the vast expanse of woodland in the English lines. The prevailing note is not brilliancy of colour, and those who represent Peshawar with a wealth of various pigments simply supply us with a creation of their own imagining. Its dominating colour is a monotonous and unvarying dun, with scarcely a relieving ray of brighter hue. But watch it in the early morning, when a gossamer haze of dusty cloud gives a softness and a mystery to every pinnacle and every cupola, and makes them shine with a pale iridescence. You will then find the old city of Peshawar, with its crumbling mud-walls, its shapeless roofs, its strange medley of disordered edifices, surpassingly beautiful as it rises above its girdle of slumbering trees and wide-stretching meadows, and with the stately rampart of mountains standing round in the hazy distance. Brightness of colour would only bring incongruity into the picture.

It is typical of the existing régime that a Hindu shrine of some note lies amidst a grove of palm-trees close below us, a centre of reverence for the minority of that religion, and secure from attack by a preponderating population of fervent Mussulmans. Whatever lies but little below the surface, there is order now to all outward seeming.

In Peshawar accident gave us an experience of an Indian up-country inn, which is an instructive variation from the constant hospitality dealt out to the guest from England. One inn may count as a type of many, and I am not disposed to think hotel life in India so bad as it is reported. The hotel is occupied chiefly by more or less permanent residents, and would not thrive upon its casual guests. The hotels are all built upon one model. The offices are in the middle, and the hotel is a one-storied building, standing in a pleasant compound, and surrounded by a verandah, upon which every chamber opens. For the truckle bed the visitor supplies his own blankets and pillows, and generally his sheets. Behind it lies the dressing-room and separate bathroom. The rooms are all identical, with bare walls reaching some 15 or 16 feet high, getting their light and ventilation from small windows high aloft, as in a prison cell. The furniture is scanty, and if you wish a sitting-room, as permanent residents naturally do, you obtain it by converting a bedroom into a sitting-room by banishing the bed. The public rooms consist of a dining-room and a bare and rather empty sitting-room, which is usually deserted. The guests' names appear on a list in the verandah, and any caller looks for the guest he wishes to see by pushing aside the straw blind that serves for a door to his room. The rule is simple and the life far from luxurious; but the essentials of comfort are there. I am not disposed to think that an attempt to imitate the luxuries of modern hotels would materially improve hotels in India.

Life at Peshawar is pleasant; but a more exciting experience awaits us in the journey up the Khyber Pass.

VI

ON THE AFGHAN FRONTIER

IN CAMP AT BALABGAHR,
DELHI DISTRICT, *November* 27, 1907.

IT was an early morning last week when, in a little one-horse tumtum, with a second horse harnessed at the side to serve as companion and to give an occasional helpful pull in ascending hills, we started along the nine miles of level road that lead out from Peshawar to Jumrud Fort. In appearance our horses are not much to look at, but they make the pace through the shady roads of the English lines and out to the far-stretching plain beyond, covering the nine miles in little more than an hour. Already there are many natives afoot, and isolated groups are passing that are to swell the aggregate of some caravan, or khafila, that is to make its way up the Pass, on this one of the two days in the week when our pickets are out and the road is fairly secure. At Jumrud, which stands at the entrance of the defile piercing the great rampart of grim mountains that have faced us since we left Peshawar, all is stir and bustle. The officers and men of the Khyber Rifles—the Militia force, composed mostly of Afridis, which guards the Pass—are busy arranging, as best they may, the motley crowds of the caravans. Our business there is soon arranged, and with an armed Sepoy of the regiment as our escort, we start again up the Pass. We have scarcely left the fort when we overtake a huge caravan proceeding up the road. A vast crowd of human beings, hundreds of gigantic Bactrian camels, interspersed with countless donkeys, stretch along the road in our front farther than the eye can reach. The scene is a weird one. On either side rise the mountains, bare and stony, except for little, round, isolated trees, studded over them at regular distances. My own companions are the Pathan driver and the Pathan escort, and with them my few Hindustani words would be useless. The vast shouting assemblage, the wrangling and crushing and jostling, sound and look more threatening than they really are; because, in truth, the caravan is bent on its own business, and there is nothing more than the usual excited jargon of a motley crowd who probably speak a dozen different tongues. The huge camels, with manes like lions and great hairy legs, look worse than they are, and give no signs of the fierceness with which they are sometimes credited. The cries of the driver and the armed escort sufficed to secure us a passage of a sort, with only one mishap, the breaking of the iron span to which the traces of our second horse were fastened, and which was patched up after a fashion with a rotten bit of rope. The crowd of human beings was stranger even than the camels that bore them. On the back of each camel, besides huge loads of various goods, there were perched families of women and small children with long dark hair, high foreheads, hooked noses, and eyes glistening like beads, balancing themselves with perfect ease and confidence on their lofty seats. The donkeys, in addition to their other loads, generally carried a thriving brood of hens and chickens, which seemed as well accustomed to this mode of travelling as their masters, and were perfectly undisturbed by all the shouting and pushing in the narrow road.

At intervals along the road we pass the little pickets of the Khyber Rifles, perched on some eminence a few hundred yards off, and turning out, as we pass each of them, to salute a Sahib's equipage. Here and there we come across a group of Afridis on the road, all armed but peaceable, and occasionally we see one ploughing, or tending sheep, with a gun slung upon his shoulders. On the other days of the week they might not be so pleasant to encounter, but now they seem as peaceably inclined as if they carried their guns only for sport. Practically, the whole population is not only Mussulman, but fanatically keen for their religion. We meet a few privileged Hindus who have business in the country; but they are always to be distinguished by the red stripes which run along their trousers, and which show that they have the privilege of passage.

We have not gone far before we meet another caravan, longer even than the first, and this time descending from Afghanistan. The process of penetrating an oncoming mass is worse, if anything, than that of passing ahead of one that is going in our own direction; but, bar the shouting, and occasional pushes from the camels and their burdens, it is accomplished with good-humour and without any serious mishap. A serious dispute would, in the circumstances, have been inconvenient. About half-way the Pass narrows to a deep ravine between precipitous rocks, and in its centre rises the Fort of Ali Masjid, standing on an eminence, with the small white mosque from which it takes its name lying at its foot. The road is admirably constructed, but it is often steep enough to try the nerves, and on one side there is generally a precipitous descent. Our pony—because, in the descents, the function of the second is altogether superfluous—rattles down at a great pace, and one cannot help thinking what would be the certain result of a single stumble, or of any failure in the harness or the shafts, which are not of a kind to inspire entire confidence in their security. After that a long and almost level road brings us to the Fort of Landi Kotal, built in a bare, sandy, treeless basin surrounded by hills, and with only a few fort-like habitations of family communities, each enclosed in a high mud-wall, and with its outlook tower—for purposes of offence as well as defence.

Life in that distant fort must be trying enough, especially when the little group of English officers is reduced—as occasionally happens—to a minimum. Coming from the centre to the very extremity of the Empire, where our authority tapers away almost to vanishing point, one cannot help wondering whether at home we duly estimate the conditions of life in such outposts; whether we appreciate the indomitable pluck that such a position demands; above all, whether we are quite careful enough that the nerves of Empire should have sufficient sustenance to give force to their extremities. Here there is no polo and no amusement. The officer cannot go out shooting without an escort, and then only to a limited distance. No one can leave the fort unarmed, and in a walk of a mile or two to the top of Pisgah Hill (as it is called), with the officer in command, we had to be accompanied by an armed escort. The people about were pleasant enough in manner, and greeted us cheerily in a Pushtu phrase, meaning "May you not be tired." But the ice is very thin that covers the depths of possible danger below the surface. The Khyber Rifles (called in joke the "Catch 'em Alives") are bright and good-tempered fellows, generally with a merry grin on their faces. But they have family links with all the fighting tribes amongst the hills, and family complications might make loyalty to discipline difficult at a pinch. We may play the game of hazard a little too long. Meanwhile, apart from the hazards of supine inaction, are we counting its cost? Do we take stock of the valuable lives, a goodly national asset, lost in little nameless skirmishes amongst a population that would almost welcome the intervention of the hand of order and authority? Do we remember the loss of prestige incurred by failure to protect friendly tribes against the ravages of their enemies? Do we count what it would cost, in the event of serious warfare, to maintain communications through these regions, which might now, at comparatively little cost or fighting, be reduced to order, and afford a safe line of advance?

From Pisgah Hill we looked down—it seemed almost a stone's-throw—upon the nullah that forms the boundary of Afghanistan. About the possession of the nullah itself, I believe, there is some dispute. Beyond that point no stranger can go without a special permit from the Amir, except at the risk of his life. We saw a few Afghan forts, the cantonments near Jellalabad, and the River Cabul running below the hills. We have come to the very extreme edge of our power and influence, and beyond it we are looking upon what is to all intents and purposes a barbarous Empire. If current belief amongst its neighbours be true, the methods of Afghan administration would have been congenial to the most ruthless of mediæval despots. Blood-curdling as these reports are, they cannot be denied the merit of a certain picturesqueness of refined cruelty.

The view of Afghanistan does not end the interest of what we see from Pisgah Hill. Beyond the nearer ranges and far to the north, on our right hand, we see the snow-tipped hills of Chitral. On the left, across the intervening hills of the irreconcilable Zakka Khels of the Bazaar Valley, who sorely need a lesson of police, we see the tops of the mountains which close in the Peiwar Pass, where part of the advance was made in 1878. It is a question how long we can, with due regard either to our duties in maintaining the Pax Britannica or the security of our Empire, disregard the necessity of pacifying this region of the Tirah. The task will not be made the easier by delay. But only long experience, and the spirit, at once alert and prudent, which the Warden's life engenders, can tell when it has come to be just the right moment to strike home. The problem is too hard for the recklessness of a traveller's hasty judgment.

It is necessary to be back at Jumrud before dark — and, apart from all undesirable encounters, the road is scarcely one that a traveller would care to traverse except in daylight—so our stay at Landi Kotal could not be more than three hours. On the return journey I had the advantage of the company of one of our officers, and his explanations vastly increased the interest of the road. Our authority, such as it is, extends only to a few yards on either side of the road. Any attempt to penetrate the ravines on either side might have troublesome consequences. The feuds between the families on either side are constantly breaking out. As we drove down we met a non-commissioned officer of the Khyber Rifles, who, while at home on furlough shortly before, had been wounded while sitting in front of his own house, quite near the road, by an enemy who was watching him from the stronghold of his family close by. The shot would not probably have been fired on the road, and there he might be safe enough ; but we saw the deep cutting which he had made from the road to his house, a couple of hundred yards off, to enable him to reach his house in safety. At another point in the route, a little farther on, we came to a bank near the road where a toothless and decrepit old villain, who enjoys the euphonious name of Tarsa Gul, or the Fresh Rose, seats himself daily to watch the travellers as they pass. He is credited with a long catalogue of murders and disorders, and came to possession of his present little dominion by the murder of a brother's widow and all her family. Doubtless his present dependants congratulate themselves on being free from the tyrannous despotism of British rule. Insurance premiums should rule high amongst his subjects.

When we drop down to Jumrud the evening is already closing in, and we cover at a good pace the remaining nine miles of level road to Peshawar. The officer who gave us his company to Jumrud is obliged to stay there on duty, and is disappointed—a disappointment accepted without grumbling—of a night amid the social pleasures of the English lines. It gives one a home-like feeling to pass once more under the shady avenues past the Club, and in amongst the bungalows and gardens. In less than twelve hours one has had an experience such as lasts a lifetime. Late in the evening we are off again in the train, on the return journey southwards. Most of the journey is made in darkness over country that we had already seen. In the morning we are again running down amongst the crumbling sandhills that mark the rise to the Rawal Pindi plain from the south, then across the Jhelum and the Chenab, which look broad and prosperous enough amidst the general drought. Then down farther, following the course of the never-ending Grand Trunk road, with its broad avenues, and its slowly creeping lines of camels and of ox-carts; and so past the Shahdara Gardens, over the Ravi, with its bridge of boats and its expanse of sand, and once again across the woodland glade that stretches under the walls of Lahore Fort.

VII

OFFICIAL CAMP LIFE IN A DELHI DISTRICT

November 30, 1907.

WHATEVER may be said of travelling in India, there is one thing on which it is possible to speak with some certainty: the traveller will never, if he is capable of making any estimate at all, meet with that most irksome of all travelling recompenses—disappointment. The fastidious may affect to despise what he sees; the reckless may criticise; the modest traveller may be overwhelmed by the vastness of the scene and its boundless problems; but no one can fail—and all the less as he may have tried to study its history, or have been in touch at a distance with Anglo-Indian life—to feel that he is here brought into contact with the mightiest contrast between his own past experiences and all that he now sees before him. One wonders all the more that those who have spent long years in the service of India can settle back into the ordinary conditions of life at home, can subscribe to our conventions, and sympathise with our everyday interests, and yet keep at the back of their minds that strange scene which has passed every day before them, in which they have personally formed a living and active force, and into the depths of which even they have never been able fully to penetrate. However we may be affected we must feel that here we are face to face with a strange and unfamiliar world; and its impression may be even more vivid for us who come to it with a lifetime of commonplace experience behind us. Its colour, its variety, its dramatic contrasts; the infinite pathos of the life that passes before him as it were in a silent show—all these may produce various impressions on the traveller, but never that of disappointment that the magnitude of the contrast is less than he expected, or that there is less to be seen and studied than he had anticipated. This is the spirit of the scene, and its outward accessories play up so well to the part! It is in the jungle districts, away from the bustle of the large towns, that one sees India best. There the teeming population may be watched, in every garb, from the coarse cotton sheet which clothes the field labourer to the rich colours and materials worn by the local magnate, and with all those manifold distinctions of rank, fenced in by a hundred quaint observances which are bred in the bone, and are as little affected by Western notions of equality as the vast arid plains are touched by the few scattered water-tanks. There is movement and stir enough; the continual chatter of the camp followers; the indignant snore of the crowd of baggage camels; the cooing of pigeons; the shrill piping of the green parrots restlessly flitting amongst the trees; the rumble of ox-waggons and an occasional outbreak of barking dogs, or, by night, the yelp of jackals. But, folding it all in, there is a sense of supreme and overmastering silence and calm, which seems to rest upon all the lesser sounds and movements, and only to be made more impressive by their petty interruptions. The spirit of rural India stages itself effectively.

After returning for a few hours to Lahore, which has already made itself something of a home, I passed on to Delhi a few days ago. For the first time in my experience the railway journey was made in fairly comfortable conditions. One can hardly but have his feelings stirred as he approaches a spot so rich in memories as Delhi. As we draw near the city the first view is that of the long stretch of the Jumna, with its wide sandy banks, where the native dhobies are busy over their washing. Then we have an impression of hazy sunshine; then an expanse of barrack grounds; then a big bridge over the river; a tract of dusty plain, and then the station. Leaving it, our first sight of Delhi is the Chandi Chauk or "Silver Market," with all its wealth of foliage and its busy booths; then the huge Mosque with its perfection of simple and yet stately outline; then the Fort with its rampart of Agra red-stone, battered by the guns that played upon it during the Mutiny; then the Cashmere Gate, with all its stirring memories; then the Flagstaff Tower, with its grim tragedy of fifty years ago; and then the Ridge over which our troops advanced on their historic task; then the wide expanse of woodland beyond which the British camp lay before the siege, and where, under altered conditions, the great Durbar was lately held. Our first view was a short one, and it could hardly have had a better standpoint than that of the Circuit House, built for the Viceroy and his guests during that Durbar. I hope to see more of Delhi later.

Early the next morning we started for camp under the best and kindest of auspices, and no experience could be better for one who wishes to judge the realities of Anglo-Indian administration than life in the camp of a great official—especially when host and hostess add long and sympathetic experience of the country to the most gracious hospitality, and to a community of association in Scottish memories and traditions. A week in camp under such guidance gives more than years of reading.

The accessories of the camp are themselves a source of endless interest. We travel with some scores of attendants, each with his own special duties which can in no way be infringed upon or intermingled. There are between forty and fifty baggage camels, who are a study in themselves. There is an irresistible mixture of dignity and affectation in their deportment. All day long, and more especially when they are being loaded, they indulge in a chorus of dissatisfaction, something between a snort and a snore, half indignant and half plaintive, and when they proceed on the march it is with an air of supreme disdain, affecting *naso suspendere adunco* all the world and their surroundings in particular. They step slowly as if they despised the earth they trod upon, and the nose-string adds to the absurd effect by its likeness to the cord of a monocle. Early each morning we ride on to the next stage, to find a new camp already pitched; because there is always a relay of tents which are used on alternate nights. In this, the cool weather season, the morning air is crisp and exhilarating, and we have reached the new camp before the mid-day sun has attained his full force. The whole big arrangement—the bandobast (or bundobust) as it is called—works with the precision wrought out of long experience. At intervals along our ride we make detours to visit an outlying village or two, where we are met by bodies of the villagers, headed by their lumbadar or headsman, and our cavalcade is joined by the principal native officers on horseback. The Financial Commissioner is accompanied by the English officers of the district, the Commissioner or Deputy-Commissioner, the Settlement Officer, and any Assistant Commissioners in the locality. The subjects of investigation are infinite in their variety. He and his subordinates unite in themselves the duties of supervisors of settlement work, of surveyors of taxes, of remitters of taxation which a bad harvest makes impossible of payment, of agents of precautionary measures against the plague, of investigators of titles and the relations between landlord and tenant. They dole out loans of eight rupees and upwards, to the amount of many thousands, and have to satisfy themselves that the loan is required, and that the security is fair. They superintend irrigation work, and see how far it accomplishes its ends. All complaints and grievances are patiently heard, and the measures of defence against famine are carefully provided for. The elders of each village squat round the carpet, where the Commissioner sits before his office tent, and volubly propound their views. Each has his proper place assigned; and if any one possesses the highly prized privilege of having a chair at such a conference, he presents his certificate, and the honour is duly accorded. It is easy to see how such ceremony harmonises with all the feelings of the group. The business may be various enough. Now a new rat-trap has to be inspected, and now a scheme to be devised for overcoming some racial prejudice against necessary measures of plague precaution. A dispute about well-water, a grievance against a mortgagee, a case of landlord oppression—each has its place. Any defect in canal irrigation is brought forward, and the aid of the Commission invoked. The scene is not without its humorous incidents. An excited beggar is clamorous for his share of any loan that is going, although he has no interest in crops or seeds. Without violence or hustling, he is quietly persuaded to stand aside, and submits with a smile as if he saw the humour of the situation. At times a speaker, who carries no weight with his fellows, interposes, and he is quietly waved to silence by a sweep of his neighbour's arm. The Hindu has no consuming prejudice in favour of truth, and his politeness tempts him to answer vaguely, and as he thinks his interlocutor desires, but in presence of his fellow-villagers he does not dare to misrepresent the facts in his own interest. All have their hearing, and when matters have been settled we pass on amidst profound salaams. We are here beyond the farthest influence of the wildest native press, and the propaganda of the most fervent agitators. One influence alone has deserved and earned their absolute trust—the conviction that unwavering and impartial justice has been meted out to them. If they have complaints against native officials, they know that they will be listened to and not summarily dismissed. They are voluble and quick in reply; content to trust authority that has won their respect; impressionable like children, and conscious of their own powerlessness to help themselves. To judge them or their condition by our maxims of the West is mere moonstruck madness. Here we are in a typical sub-district, forming about a fifth of the district under a Commissioner, which is itself something like a fifth of the whole Punjab Province. The population is about 700,000, and it is divided into some 1200 villages, with an average population of about 600 each. The whole of this population is under some three English officials, who have to guide its welfare with parental care. There are many native officials—some satisfactory enough, but hardly with that standard of official purity which prevails amongst the Anglo-Indian Civil Service, and is the very instinct of their life and work. That there are petty oppression and petty exactions amongst these lower officials is indubitable; and complaints, which timidity rarely permits, have to be carefully investigated. Every detail of administration has to be examined, and every remission of taxation has to be made known to villagers who only dimly understand the vast system that labours unrestingly for their good. Can we parallel such magnitude of work entrusted to so small a band?

For such work as this there is one essential and fully established principle, which is the foundation of the whole system. There is one mark which distinguishes this from almost any other country—we might say from every other country not under British rule. No one engaged in the administration can have the most remote personal interest in the questions which he has to settle. Elsewhere we meet men who have great business interests to push, who are studying commercial prospects, who have to exploit the land they live in for purposes of trade. We meet no such class in rural India. Every one who exercises any authority here is detached from material interests in a way which is inconceivable at home or in our colonies; and without such absolute detachment they could win the confidence of no Hindu.

But, besides this, there is need of infinite patience, of deep-rooted self-control, of a fund of sympathy that is cautious of betraying or of cheapening itself by any outward show of sentiment. That would very quickly exhaust its own resources, and dissipate its authority, like water poured in handfuls upon these dusty plains.

As one watches the work of this small *posse* of high officials, one sees also other ingredients that go to make them what they are. After details have been investigated, broad principles have to be considered, and the ultimate economical effect of each decision has to be weighed. The readiest solution is not always that which will rest upon the most secure foundation. It is not startling ingenuity or quickness of device that is most required, but rather patience, calmness, and measured judgment. It is when active steps have to be taken in an emergency that promptness is required; and hence the need of prudent foresight and deliberate precaution. Each officer must make himself master of the Famine Code, and know beforehand all the immediate steps which long experience prescribes in the event of famine appearing. For the signs of that appearance he must watch with an alert and patient eye, which suffers no symptom to escape his observation.

It is not difficult to appreciate the type of official that such duties, successfully discharged, tend to create. I say nothing as to the method of their original selection. But there is no object-lesson of the truth that special work creates and perfects its own best instruments so impressive as is supplied by the condition of the Indian Civil Service to-day. Personal idiosyncrasies cannot disappear, and various ranges of intelligence are seen; but they are marvellously smoothed over, and are dominated by the one impulse that stirs the whole of the vast system. Nowhere is it seen so effective as in the ever-varying but ever-strenuous work of camp life. Because it must not be supposed that the interviews and conferences I have described cover the whole business of the day. Every possible interval has to be used to transact the daily official routine. Huge files arrive each day. Opinions have to be formed on questions of large import; letters have to be drafted; pressing decisions have to be given. At least from six to seven hours of desk work must be transacted, in addition to the interviews, the hearing of complaints, and the settlement of petty local details.

There are other incidents of life in camp which engage the interest of the idle visitor. We have now had three halts—at Badarpur, at Balabgahr, and at Palwal—and at each there has been some special object of interest or some special phase of village life to see. We have seen the vast deserted town of Tuglukabad, with the ponderous tomb near by—an imposing memorial of Mussulman power long before the Mogul days, and impressive rather from its massive strength and stately proportions than from any decorative art or gracefulness of design. We have had an entertainment by moonlight from a band of village minstrels—half musical, half dramatic. I have visited a native secondary school—in gala for the occasion, when an hour or two's notice gave time for arches of honour and flags to be erected, and the scholars to be dressed in holiday attire of the most brilliant hues. I heard recitations in which, as my interpreter explained, the evils of borrowing—or *tokavi*—were forcibly depicted, and the beauties of the sunset were described, and I found geometrical propositions demonstrated according to the most approved and modern methods, with the fashionable deposition of Euclid from his place of authority. Life does not lie heavy on your hands in an Indian administrative camp.

VIII

LIFE IN AN ADMINISTRATIVE OFFICER'S CAMP

DELHI, *December* 6, 1907.

ANOTHER feature of interest in the moving life of an administrative officer's camp is found in the little townships—with some eight to twelve or thirteen thousand inhabitants—which we meet with on the route. In this part of the country there are no such things as isolated houses. The tillers of the land are gathered together in little villages or in these larger townships. These are generally at distances of a fair day's march along the ancient roads, which are marked along their course by the stately milestones, or minars, rising some twenty feet high, and serving not only to tell the progress of the traveller, but to point out to him his direction a considerable bit ahead. The townships commonly stand on an eminence, neither natural nor purely artificial, but due to the fact that the mud buildings which have formed the towns, inhabited for some thousands of years, have crumbled through successive generations, and have in their turn served as foundations for later buildings. Sometimes we come across such an eminence now tenantless, and only marked by some crumbling ruins, indicating the site of a now deserted town. The townships are generally surrounded by lofty walls, once serviceable for purposes of defence, and still seeming to give a sense of security—though but a false one—in their crumbling decay. They are entered through arched gates, often still retaining some trace of architectural pretension, and then we are in a labyrinth of narrow streets, with the open booths and workshops of every trade. Something has been done to fight against racial dislike of sanitary precautions, and every effort is made against their neglect; but the fight is a hard one. Here we have the booths—at once workshop and warehouse—of the blacksmith, the tinsmith, the coppersmith, and the dyer; the little storehouses of the grain merchants; the sweetmeat booths, which even in the dread of famine do a lively trade; the licensed retailer of bhang, who is under the strictest Government supervision, and holds a Government licence, any infringement of which would be severely punished. There is the booth where the "scutcher" of cotton plies his instrument, which in shape as well as sound is like nothing so much as a gigantic lyre. Interspersed amongst them, and under the same pall of dust, we find bigger storehouses, and occasionally houses of a slightly more substantial kind, where the well-to-do banyah amasses considerable wealth, while he lives almost as simply as his poorer neighbours. There are here and there wheel-wells, from which water for all household purposes is obtained, and we had ocular demonstration that their purity was very little regarded. In one case we saw nothing but stagnant water in a tank; but a proposal to replenish it from the canal had been vetoed, because it was "holy water," which must be tainted by no intermixture. To put disinfectants in the wells might easily raise a rumour of poisoning them, and would give a convenient weapon to the agitators. It can only be done, if done at all, with an infinity of caution.

Each township has its Hindu temples and its Mohammedan mosques, between which peace must be kept somehow, and which must not be allowed to interfere with one another's privileges. In the township school, generally a building well built and well equipped, with a considerable staff of native teachers, all creeds and castes may intermingle, although in the boarding-houses there must be separate eating-rooms for Hindu and Mussulman. The school is an object of pride to the better citizens, although the pride centres, perhaps a little too exclusively, in the gaining of high places by the selected pupils in the entrance competition at the Delhi High School, which is to carry them on to the University at Lahore. There are generally the remains of the old *seraí* or rest-house, provided in old days for the caravans, where they might pass the night in the security of common defence.

In these narrow streets, roughly paved, unlighted, buried in a thick covering of dust, and with a monotony of oppressive odour, there are by day a busy hum of business and a constant chorus of cries and gesticulations. As evening falls they become quiet, and are curtained in by a heavy pall of haze and dust. Their denizens take life as it comes, with the elixir of a sublime patience. If disease falls on them, it is the stroke of fate; and schemes for fighting it they regard at best with apathetic tolerance. If their life is to be raised, it must be by other agency than their own. Here there is none of that crowding from the country to the town which is the bugbear against which we make puny fights in the West. If we exclude the larger cities, like Lahore, Amritsar, and Delhi, probably 95 per cent. of the Punjab population are dwellers in the country villages or small towns, which are really agricultural; but the banyah of the large town stretches his spider-like claws of usury over the countryman, and the only defence against his blood-sucking lies in a parental administration which forbids the alienation of mortgaged land except with official sanction. One wonders whether an artificial system of Small Holdings would so certainly be free from a similar scourge in our own country. Here, at least, there is no lack of Small Holdings. In the Punjab, out of a population of twenty million, there are some three millions of proprietors, each with an average holding of eight acres, and only about fifty of them (apart from the independent Rajahs) pay land tax upon an income amounting to £900 a year. Yet their lot is scarcely one of unadulterated prosperity.

One of the most curious of the documents inspected at these visits of supervision is the table of the village genealogy. It is elaborately drawn up and printed on a linen sheet, which is sometimes 10 or 12 feet long. In some cases we found it went back for twenty or more generations. Each step in the descent is accurately recorded, and is familiarly known not only to every member of the family, but to all its branches. In one case we found that the genealogical table of a Jat village of some 400 inhabitants traced each man back through twenty-one generations to a single progenitor. It established for each his rights of succession in case of the failure of another branch, and served as a sort of title-deed to his actual holding. Some of the entries were tested by a careful questioning of the men selected. In not a single case did the questions reveal any doubt or hesitation as to the long table of descent, and if there were any need, the answers were supplemented by a dozen attestants. Yet they rarely could tell the actual amount of their own holding or of the taxes they paid. This table, carefully corrected and kept up to date, forms the Real Property Register. By its means disputes as to succession are settled, and quarrels and litigation are avoided. I wonder how many of our landed aristocracy could boast a genealogy so amply attested and so carefully recorded!

To-day we have reached a new camping ground at Brahminikhera, or the "Abode of the Brahmin Woman," where there is no township or village, but only one of those deserted hillocks which generations ago have been the site of a fair-sized town. A wide plain stretches round our tents, and there is nothing here of the stir and sounds of neighbouring life that meet us near any cluster of dwellings. There is less dust, and the sunset sends a clearer light across the horizon without the usual intervening haze. The whole scene is infinitely calm and peaceful, and the only sounds that reach us as darkness descends are the songs of the labourers working the machines at the wells scattered over the plain, where the bullocks are slowly drawing the wheel that brings up the *charas*, or leathern pitcher, from the depths, and empties it into the tiny channels that cross the fields; an occasional grunt from the camels kneeling about the camp fires, where their drivers are cooking their evening meal; and the faint distant cry of the jackal, strangely different from his sharp yelp by night. It is only in the official tent that the impression of restfulness is not dominant.

One or two more stages, and I have to say good-bye to this most interesting and instructive week of camp life, which has been an education in itself. I have spoken of the work as I saw it, and have described its thoroughness, its high aims, its undaunted patience, and its consummate impartiality. What am I to say of the country life itself?

The roads along which we pass are well made, and are refreshing in their umbrageous coolness and full of endless sights of interest. The green parrots are flitting, like leaves, across our path; the small grey striped squirrels scamper ceaselessly athwart the road; long trains of female labourers with their dark red drapery meet us; big herds of bullocks stroll listlessly along in charge of a small, almost naked, child, who often eases his task by lying at full length upon the back of the father of the herd; strings of camels plod along to market; and the rumbling bullock-cart passes ever and again with a whole family and its belongings. The monkeys leap from branch to branch; and here and there a toothless Fakir begs for alms. The life of rural India is gathered here, and watches the passing of the official equipage and its attending escort with a sort of apathetic respect, as if it were a vision from another world. The life is slow, patient, and monotonous, and the spirit of the soil has passed into their very fibre. The sky is an unrelieved blue; the evening lights are surpassingly beautiful; but beyond the leafy avenues that border the road, there is no beauty in the aspect of the country. It stretches in an unbroken level as far as the eye can reach, and—especially in this season of exceptional drought—there is nothing to be seen but bare brown soil, dusty and untidy mud banks dividing the fields, dry canal channels, and here and there unsightly wells, and a team of hump-backed oxen wearily tugging at the well ropes. There are no hamlets nestling by village hedgerows; no garden or flowers; nothing but a sad and unrelieved monotony of brown, with an occasional patch of green produced by artificial irrigation. "Bleak sunshine vainly shines around," nature is not smiling, and gives no sign of home-like rest, with all its calm and all its inheritance of patient toil.

At Hodal, some sixty miles to the south of Delhi, I part from that side of Indian life on my return to the city, where I am carried, in that peculiar product of India, an express train with none but third-class carriages. The scene changes with dramatic quickness. At the first station an English mine prospector accosts me with a voluble story of how he has been robbed and cheated by Portuguese officials at Goa, who have cancelled a concession after capital has been sunk in it. He is now on his way to seek redress, and in his view the Government of India has other things to do than to look into the hardships of the ryots' life. At table in the hotel at Delhi, where I spend two days before coming to the hospitable home of the Deputy-Commissioner, my neighbour is a traveller for a large firm of photographic film manufacturers, to whom India is only a vast field for commercial exploitation, and who is impatient with a Government that spends time in the country districts, and is not always available for the settlement of commercial contracts. They are, no doubt, all right in their own way, but it is no wonder that they do not feel a laborious Government sympathetic to their money-getting energy. One touches here a stratum of life cut off by an unfathomable gulf from all that I have just seen. Let us hope that there is room for all.

It is a hard task for a casual traveller, even after a week's residence, to say anything of Delhi. It is no part of my aim to give a detailed description — that is to be found in a hundred hand-books of various shapes and aims. I can speak only of the impression that it makes after its streets and its surroundings have shaken off their strangeness and become a little familiar; when its peculiar features have taken shape in one's eyes. Approach it from the surrounding country on any side, and you are faced by a huge wall of red sandstone, rising from a belt of rocky ridges, or of countless masses of crumbling ruins, and having a circumference of some fourteen miles. At various points that wall is broken by breaches that tell of desperate fighting fifty years ago. Outside the walls lie the English lines, with the usual bungalows and compounds, but with little of the restful shadiness and order of Lahore, or Rawal Pindi or Peshawar. Pass within the wall at the historic Cashmere Gate, which lies close to the Kudsia and the Nicholson Gardens in the English quarter, and you are in a quiet little suburb, every spot of which has its memories. Here is the pre-Mutiny church in a coat of garish yellow paint with rather a pretentious dome, and the old ball and cross, pierced by shell and bullet, lying at its door, and garnished by flowering plants. A few yards on we come to the remnants of the famous magazine, which heroic promptitude destroyed in the moment when it might have fallen into the hands of the mutineers, and the telegraph station, from which the urgent messages of alarm were sent in 1857. Passing under the railway bridge, we come to the broad parade ground, cleared of houses after the Mutiny, which lies between the great gate of the Fort and the towering domes and minarets of the Jumma Masjid. These two—Fort and Mosque—are the great monuments of Delhi. You pass up the vast steps which ascend to the Mosque from all its sides, and into its great courtyard; and only slowly does its colossal size and its surpassing dignity filter into your brain, and dominate you. Or, turning the other way, you pass into the Fort, and in place of the crowded buildings that once were pent within it, you see wide open spaces, disfigured by the hideous military buildings which house the handful of English soldiers in Delhi, and only by degrees are you conscious of the few remnants of inimitable beauty which remain to tell of the glories of Shah Jahan and the pride of his Court. Of late years these have been treated with wise and considerate care, and have been the object of careful and expert restoration, in which Italian skill has been employed, as it was in the original. We can see their unrivalled splendour. With no effort of ours, their dreamlike beauty impresses our consciousness; and they seem to group themselves in a sort of dream with all the splendour of the Arabian nights. But, after all, they stand isolated and bereft of their companions. Their beauty is partly that of ghostlike phantoms, standing apart in a silence where only a few generations back all was stir and life, luxury and passion, lavishness and cruelty—all the pomp of life and all its tragedy. They are safe now from ruin and devastation; but they are like lonely Peri, wistfully searching for their companions and wearing all their splendour like a robe of mourning. How they must hate the unsightly barracks that frown at them across the square! The Jumma Masjid standing in all its glory, the beauties of the Fort, a sad monument of forgotten splendour —these are the pride of Delhi. But it has interests that lie elsewhere.

From the gate of the Fort we may pass into the Chandi Chauk, or Silver Market, and there we are in the busy centre of Delhi life. It is a broad and bustling, and it ought to be a brilliant, thoroughfare. It hides behind its shabby, ill-cared-for buildings hoards of wealth that would make it again, as it has often been before, a splendid looting place. Down the centre runs a canal now covered over, and it is made green by a double row of stately trees. There are signs of busy prosperity at every corner, and the eye is never disengaged from some strange equipage or some characteristic scene. But it is all disfigured with the usual pall of dust. Eastern wealth prides itself — in its business side at least—in hiding itself from the eye. Jewellers, contractors, bankers, shipping agents, great mercantile houses — they are carrying on a vast business with every corner of the globe, but their chambers and their warehouses would disgrace the worst purlieus of Soho, and they have to be hunted out amongst noisome booths and by climbing dusty and ill-constructed staircases. So much wealth nowhere hides itself under such grim and abject exteriors. The breadth of the street; its occasional breaks, where some more imposing public building has been reared; the green of its trees; above all, the stir and bustle of its visible prosperity—these are the charms of the street. It has not even preserved its quaintness of Eastern architecture so well as some of the narrower streets that lurk behind it in the heart of the city.

That is one aspect of life in Delhi; there are others of which I shall have more to say.

IX

TWO ASPECTS OF DELHI—MEMORIES OF THE MUTINY

LAHORE, *December* 7, 1907.

IN my last letter I said that there were other aspects of Delhi that impress themselves more slowly. Let us see what these are.

Approach Delhi from which side you please, you will be struck by the vast expanse of untidiness and ruin that spreads round its splendid monuments. Slowly you begin to see the meaning of this. After all, modern Delhi, or, more properly, Shahjahanabad, or the city of Shah Jahan, is a mere modern excrescence, something less than three hundred years old, upon a boundless cemetery that stretches for some eleven miles or more. It is a charnel-house of men, of dynasties, of cities, of races, beneath which are buried the memories of thousands of years. It is a city, or rather a series of cities, of tombs. There are some six or seven cities of which only the mighty ruins remain, stretching away to the southwards, farther than the eye can reach. There are huge stately tombs at intervals of a mile or two, and between them there spreads a wilderness of solitary graves and crumbling mausoleums. We have, only two or three miles from the modern city, the great mass of Humayun's tomb—impressive from its size and stately lines, and despising tricks of ornament. A few miles farther on we have the tomb of Safdar Jang, a comparatively late construction, only some 150 years old. Both are surrounded by wide-spreading gardens, which a paternal Government has restored with reverential care. Not far from these we have the tomb of Nizamuddin, the Chisti saint of the thirteenth century, whose memory is still cherished and revered, and round whose grave a huge company of Princes and Princesses, of warriors, and saints, and poets, have chosen to be buried. We wander amid a labyrinth of ruins, interspersed with marble colonnades and shrines of delicate beauty, and find ourselves haunted by the ghosts of seven centuries, still potent in their sway over the thoughts and imagination of countless millions. There lie Nizamuddin himself, with a memory of unrivalled sanctity; Khusru, the prolific poet, the admired of the Persian Sadi, whose songs are still on the tongues of his millions of worshippers; Jahanara Begum, the favourite daughter of Shah Jahan, companion of saints, whose epitaph, written by herself, prays, "Let nothing but the grass conceal the grave of the poor and humble, the transitory Jahanara, disciple of the saints"; and a long roll of warriors and statesmen. It is a strangely moving scene: dust and ruins, lavish decoration and delicate tracery, mingled in perplexing medley. On the day when I visited it, under native escort, I was, so far as I saw, the only European amidst a crowd of many thousands of natives, who were celebrating some festival at the shrine. There were the usual bizarre and tinsel ornaments, so incongruous with the delicate artistic grace of the shrines, so ill-assorted with the grimness of the crumbling ruins all around. There was the usual crowd of suppliants at the shrine, and the usual monotonous chant of the group of musicians. All were in their gayest dresses, effective in the mass, but, taken separately, of the most ill-assorted materials and the most inharmonious and violent hues. Toys and sweetmeats were being sold close to each shrine; the passages were encumbered with squatting groups and slumbering figures. The crowd stared at a stranger, but their courtesy never failed. The descendants of those whose tombs lay round us proffered their help as guides and cicerones, and were pleased with moderate backsheesh. So far as one could see, they were a happy, frolicsome, yet courteous crowd; but how hopelessly distant were all their real thoughts from any sympathy with ours! In the midst there is a huge tank—the spring of Nizamuddin—said to be of miraculous construction, and the waters of which possess illimitable powers of cure. Its surface is of a slimy green, and its waves are not well savoured to the smell. Round it stand lofty-domed tombs and shrines, rising some sixty feet above its forty feet depths. From the topmost domes—after a place was made for me on the opposite parapet—there sprang some half-dozen youths feet foremost into its murky waters, and in an almost miraculously short space they had climbed the sixty feet of staircase, and stood beside me, in a panting and dripping row, in quest of backsheesh. The strange mixture of life and death, the glitter of the tinsel work, and the restful beauty of the shrines, the dusty, crumbling ruins, and the intervals of fresh-coloured delicate tracery and inlaid incrustations, the merry junketing, and the background of fervent religious feeling—all passed before me as a dream rather than a reality. The general impression was all: the details were blurred and mingled; but the picture was none the less effective.

It is no part of my plan to give a description in detail of the site and remains of the various Delhis, which one after another have been abandoned, and now raise their gaunt and dusty ruins over the vast plain that stretches south of modern Delhi. There is Indrapat, which we pass on the way to Nizam-uddin, which boasts of Hindu origin, and where the more ornamental brick gates of the

Mogul are inserted into much more ancient walls. It is a stately ruin, and is now occupied, like many of the old city walls, by a Hindu village, which conceals itself behind the ancient fortifications. The most imposing of all, Tuglukabad, dates from the fourteenth century, and was formed in a passing whim by a bloodthirsty tyrant, who defended himself behind what are far the most stupendous ramparts which I have yet seen in India. A curse lay upon the place from the first. Tugluk was regarded with detestation by the Saint Nizamuddin, who prophesied that his proud city would either be desolate or the abode of Gojars—a low caste of cowherds. Its day was but a brief one; and now within its walls, with their circuit of four miles, there is at this day a village of Gojars. The prophecy doubtless worked its own accomplishment, and a custom, once established, is not easily abandoned in India.

But the most supremely interesting of all these remains, august amid all their ruin, is Purana Delhi, or old Delhi, eleven miles out of the modern city. It dates its origin back to a Hindu dynasty, and in its proudest age its stately edifices were raised by Kutab-uddin and Alai-uddin—great leaders in Mogul annals. The circumstance of chief interest about it is that Kutab-uddin, in the construction of his great mosque, employed, and at the same time defaced, the remnants of a Hindu temple. The treasures of a hundred shrines of an alien faith were torn from their sites, and either contemptuously buried amidst the foundations of the mosque or employed in its decoration. Part of the new building was reared on the pillars of the Hindu temple, with their marvellous carvings, and its sculptures were built into the walls, and then covered with plaster to hide their hated symbols. The mosque has fallen into ruin. Only fragments, and here and there a mighty gateway, adorned with delicate sculpture, and entrancing us by its wondrous mingling of marble and redstone carving, remain to tell us of its former magnificence and of its spacious pride. But the plaster has fallen from the pillars. Their quaint carvings are revealed; and in a strange medley the symbols of Hindu and Mohammedan worship are blended together in this mighty ruin.

One miracle of beauty—to my mind, the chief pride of Delhi and its neighbourhood—still stands practically intact—the Kutab Minar, or tower of Kutab. Of all the monuments of Mogul art that I have yet seen, this has impressed me most. It rises some 240 feet, tapering from a base of some 50 feet in diameter, to a summit of less than 10 feet. At intervals it is broken by the five storeys, each of which is marked by a graceful balustrade, and towards the summit the marble predominates over the redstone of which it is constructed, and thus adds to its lightness and its flowerlike grace. It is strange, and to Western eyes, at first, bizarre. But it emerges with such consummate grace from the massive ruins around us, it seems at once so delicate and so strong, that the rich incrustation of its decorations and the marvellous beauty of its colouring compel our submissive admiration. It shakes away from its feet all the dust and crumbling ruins round it which tell of mingled faiths and centuries of bloodshed. It remains a tall and solitary flower of surpassing beauty, rising proudly, and with all the brilliancy of springtime, from the dusty, withered, and decayed plants that spread in desolate confusion round its feet.

And what must it mean to all those thousands who to-day crowd into this historic stage, live through their obscure existence, pass and repass amid the shadows of these tombs of the past? None of the traditions of these ruins has faded from their memories. The tombs are guarded by those who claim, on good grounds, kinship with the founders of these splendid relics. Fable and tradition, memories of old dynasties, the mystic symbols of religion—all are as real to them as they were of old. They mingle together now, Hindu and Mussulman, sharing in the same festivals, bound by the same love of religious mysticism, only superficially touched by contact with the Western spirit. They must feel that they live amongst the ruins of a tragic past of struggle and of cruelty. In this vast sink of contention, no real national spirit has been evolved. They are the product of all these centuries of ceaseless strife and ruthless tyranny; and from it all they have learned infinite patience, inbred habits of submission, apathy and lack of energy, and ingrained aptitude for obedience to authority, broken only by passionate obedience to custom, and by a potentiality of blind religious zeal. To them our rule must seem a couch of restful ease after the nightmare of centuries of tragedy. It is only by the simple directness of its aim, by its quiet assertion of authority, by its undeviating rectitude of justice, by its slow persuasiveness, that our rule can preserve its hold. It is to them a dream of infinite restfulness, whatever the hardships of their lonely life may be. How terrible the responsibility of any reckless words, any hare-brain schemes, that would break the spell, and let loose once more the flood-gates of strife, and anarchy, and religious fanaticism!

This is one aspect of Delhi and its environs. Turn to the north of the city, and we are amidst other memories and far different scenes. Northwards there lie none of the shrines and tombs that make the plain to the south one vast cemetery. Pass from the Cashmere Gate out towards the famous Ridge beyond, and the memories stirred are those of fifty years ago. We see the ruined bastions broken in the cannonade of 1857. In the Kudsia Gardens we find, carefully marked, the site of the batteries which crept closer and closer to the walls; the bridge to the gate, which was won by consummate heroism. Across the road we see the statue of John Nicholson, the prime hero of the siege, who fell in the hour of victory. Before us lies the red Flagstaff Tower, where the refugees crowded in hourly expectation of death; and we are on the Ridge over which the British Army advanced, and beyond which its first portion waited for the supporting columns to gather. We see studded along the plain those "Bells of Arms," which rise at intervals like block-houses, where the rifles of the native regiments were stored. The very air is redolent of the tragedy which is only half a century old.

This is the second aspect of Delhi. It is there that the story of the Mutiny affects us as in no other city that I have yet seen. And, beyond all question, these memories strike a stranger as being yet a living force in Delhi. Insensibly they are present in the mind of every dweller there. They recur in conversation, as they do nowhere else where I have yet been. Delhi has waxed wealthy in trade and commerce. She is a congeries of various races and creeds, and it may be, as some think, that dangerous elements have there become weaker, and that, degraded from her old dignity as the centre of Indian Empire, she is no longer a serious menace to our authority. She has now but a small military force; and it may be that this is justified. Of that I can say nothing. But I am certain of my own impression, that the Mutiny is still a living memory there. It comes across one at every turn. Each spot has its story of heroism and of tragedy, of rescue and death, or worse. It is not a fancy that leads close observers to mark amongst the outlying zemindars and in the scattered villages traces of English origin amidst the children of native families. In the early days of the tragedy English girls disappeared. Who can say what their fate may have been, and how their blood survives amidst those who for a brief moment were free from our authority, and who may have taken them for their own—to lose, in alien surroundings, the very sense of their own origin?

This is my second impression of Delhi. More circumscribed in its stage, with less of mystery, and none of the spectral gloominess of the vast cemetery that stretches to the south, it yet strikes one's heart with a nearer and more penetrating tragedy. In May last the ill-advised cackle of a native, presumably friendly, and fussily eager to gain credit for his friendliness, went far to produce something like a scare amidst an European population immersed in business, and scarcely possessing the *sang-froid* and restraint of an official and military class. Guns were fetched; games were broken up; and a perturbed assemblage of armed citizens gathered at the club. A spark might easily have set the powder ablaze. Happily, the cool judgment and the saving humour of those in authority preserved themselves from the infection of alarm, and the city from serious danger. Bogus stories of murdered Europeans and plundered houses soon proved to be a myth. But I am not disposed to blame too severely those in whom the memories of fifty years ago had bred some alarm, and who resolved to arm themselves betimes. Happily no one was one whit the worse of the few hours of nervousness.

I had an opportunity of seeing other sides of Delhi life and administration—a quiet, business-like meeting of the Reformatory Committee, where European officials and missionaries sat in conclave with native gentlemen, and engaged in a common scheme of reclamation. Results were promising on the whole, although the turbulence of the raw material was proved by the fact that in the previous week one youthful inmate had killed another with a garden implement, incensed at being addressed by the opprobrious name of "conjuror." I saw the prison, with its carpet factory, and its usual atmosphere of serene and healthful rest. I saw a sitting of the local Court, where a busy administrator employed the intervals between perplexing executive business in hearing a nice point of law, ably argued by native pleaders, who joined in the earnest wish that the Magistrate should himself give a decision and save further appeal. This unresting activity, this ungrudging help freely given in every direction to social improvement and the settlement of local disputes, presented an aspect of life in sharp contrast to the long centuries of struggle and the memories of more recent tragedy.

X

ANGLO-INDIAN SOCIETY: ITS TONE AND CONDITIONS

LAHORE, *December* 14, 1907.

BEFORE I leave Delhi there is one scene that calls for some description. It was a performance of a musical comedy by a native travelling company, and some of its features were of peculiar interest. It was, or professed to be, an original play, and the staging was more than creditable. It opened with an imposing scene representing the Durbar of a native King discussing a project of war, which is presently carried out. To prevent any excess of solemnity, there was enough of by-play carried on by the Court fool, who travestied the warlike pride of the troops on the march, and enacted a comic interlude during the fighting. There were two murders, the dramatic justice of which prevented them from being taken too seriously; and another attempted murder, which was averted by comic intervention on the part of the leading comedian. There were the usual reminiscences from Shakespeare—Dromio's denial of the receipt of the bag of gold, from the *Comedy of Errors*, and Olivia's wooing of Viola in her male attire, by the sending of a ring, from *Twelfth Night*. The singing started in the painfully high-pitched key which one always hears in India, with the result that, as the play ran its long course, one singer after another gradually lost his voice. All the women parts were taken by men or boys. The drop-scene was a curious medley of Venice and Amsterdam; and a railway accident, which was announced in the programme as of thrilling excitement, was enacted on a scale that might have suited a Lilliputian magic-lantern show. But the really odd features were something apart from all these. The faces of every actor and of all the chorus were painted to represent European complexions, and so well painted as, at first sight, completely to deceive. The delusion was helped by hands being painted as well as faces. The result was to show how easy it is to exaggerate what we take to be characteristic differences of feature, and how much we are influenced by difference of colour. Amongst the crowd of faces on the stage there were many which one would have called distinctly English in type, when the bar of complexion was removed. The only exceptions to this false complexion were some actors who took the parts of Mohammedans or Eurasians; they were pourtrayed in the colour of their own skin.

But the funniest thing of all was the real humour which occasionally appeared—all the more true because it sometimes had the native for its victim. There was a scene in a railway station that was supremely amusing. A typical English guard hustled the natives about in realistic style, and finally reduced the pride of a youthful native of self-assumed importance. The wordy war was composed by the appearance of a still more typical Eurasian station superintendent, who, with a pacific aspect and behind a pair of spectacles, lectured the guard in broken

English upon the necessity "of showing all patience and consideration to the natives, and not permitting himself any physical violence." Possibly any satiric touches against the Sahibs were toned down in consideration of our presence, which was expected and prepared for; but, in any case, there is no lack of humour in a race that can turn the laugh upon itself. The pourtrayal of a young Nawab who affected English fashions was still more laughable. He appeared, with his Court round him, in an audience chamber like a railway waiting-room, attired in a suit of knickerbockers of startling hue, with stockings of a marvellous check, and yellow shoes of unexampled brilliancy. His "sporting coat" was of the roughest tweed, and round his neck he wore—several rows of pearls! A band of minstrels and a troupe of Nautch girls were introduced with awkwardness of gesture and an affected clumsiness of instrument that were plainly meant for a burlesque; and the Anglified Nawab turned upon his sofa with an air of supreme disgust that might have been copied from Mayfair.

The performance was painfully long. It

began immediately after our arrival, a few minutes past nine, and was still going strong when we left at half-past twelve. But it was kept up with plenty of zest throughout. No list of actors was given, and they were not named upon the bills; but the chief comedian had indubitable comic gifts, and—barring the language—would make his fortune on the London boards. Indeed, it was difficult to believe that he had not himself watched those French or English models whose tricks of manner and expression he reproduced so well. To the eye—and, as I was told on good authority, to the ear as well—there was not one word of vulgarity or coarseness; and if one's tympanum could only get accustomed to the excruciating *altos*, the singing was fair enough. The accessories were sometimes amusing in themselves. The orchestra was composed of a native in full native costume, who, on one side of the stage, kept up an almost perpetual accompaniment by thumping two small drums; and of a very degraded form of harmonium played on the other side by a seedy-looking black gentleman, arrayed in a puggaree, a Highland cloak, a pair of trousers of doubtful hue, and a steel watch-chain. His expression varied from a look of languid weariness to a smile of contemptuous disdain. The play seemed to be favourably received by a pretty large audience, and I can answer for it that it had at least one most interested spectator who did not feel that the time had been ill-spent in witnessing an entirely new phase of Indian mood and character. It was odd to watch it, with all its little touches of modern humour mixed with childish simplicity, here in the midst of Delhi's busy life, the sad-faced and remote-eyed crowds of its poor, and the crumbling monuments of its tragic past.

To be back in Lahore once more seems almost like home-coming. Its buildings and its monuments have thrown off their first novelty; the labyrinth of its roads has lost its intricacy, and the various houses have begun to associate themselves with their hospitable occupiers. Insensibly one begins to learn the ways of life of the Anglo-Indian and to observe how it differs from our own.

First, as regards the houses. Every house stands in a spacious compound of its own, with a considerable expanse of lawn and flower-bed, and a long row of huts where the native servants live. There is a goodly troop of them; for even a moderate household cannot have less than from fifteen to twenty. Each has his own allotted work, which must not be in any way infringed upon. Each has his grade in a long scale, and would be grievously insulted were he asked to do the work of the grade below. One man may do a certain part of waiting at table, but he would degrade himself were he to hand you any meat. A man may brush your clothes who would not for a moment sweep the floor. The gardener would not be expected to sweep the paths. A horse often requires two syces, besides a man who cuts grass for him. Your bearer will not bring you water, but invokes the aid of the *Bhishti* (or "heavenly one"), who holds a low grade in the hierarchy. More menial duties still fall to the *Mehter* ("prince"), as the sweeper is humorously styled. Each household must have its *dhursi*, or sewing-man, and its *dhobi*, or washer-man. It is no extravagance, but dire necessity, that compels the Anglo-

Indian to surround himself with a long retinue, who live with their families within his compound.

The general type of house — from which there are rarely any marked variations — is easily described. It is something like a huge square box, one tall storey in height, stuccoed in white or colour, and with more or less of ornament in the shape of a large *porte cochere*, and a verandah which runs all round the house, and is shut in by movable blinds of straw. No windows are visible; but in a huge lid-like projection, which rises in the midst of the flat roof, you see some small apertures which serve to give light to the lofty rooms, which are rarely less than fifteen or twenty feet high. All the rooms enter off the central hall. Each sleeping-room has its separate dressing-room and bathroom—a little walled-off space on the brick floor with its water pipe and drain hole opening into the verandah. Once you get used to it there is nothing more simple and yet more comfortable than this arrangement of the rooms, from which there is rarely the smallest deviation. The kitchen is in a little annexe a few yards off, so that the smell of cooking never offends the nostrils nor adds to the burden of the hot weather season. With these dusty roads, the broiling sun, and the long distances, life to an European is impossible without some equipment of horse and tum-tum or gig. When you wish more you summon a "phitton-gharri"—rather a lumbering barouche drawn by two horses generally a good deal the worse for the wear, driven by a turbaned *sawar*, and attended by a ragged footboy, who curls himself up in the hay-net behind and, on very little provocation, goes to sleep.

It is no business of mine to discuss the social tone of Anglo-Indian society and to pass judgment on its supposed idiosyncrasies as depicted by novelists. I would not do so if I could, and I could not if I would. Only its outer aspects come within my observation. One peculiarity at once strikes the dweller at home. The general standard of living is almost identical, and there is none of that wide difference of means which is the perplexity of London life. Very few who live and work in India are possessed of large private means. Every one knows his neighbour's income, and extravagant living would only make a man ridiculous. One has 1000 rupees a month; another has 4000; but difference in social duties—which are well defined—in the size of a family, in thrift and good management, and in the expenses of education at home, very largely equalise these minor differences, so small in comparison with the gulf which separates the professional man of moderate income from the great capitalist at home. The latter class is absolutely non-existent here amongst Anglo-Indians, outside the three great cities of Bombay, Calcutta, and Madras.

Another salient feature is that life here is much more in common, and in the open air, than with us. Anglo-Indians constantly tell you that society is becoming greatly more mixed; but to eyes accustomed to home conditions, it is still singularly uniform, and a tone of happy *camaraderie* is the dominant note. Of course there are more or less close intimacies of friendship. But all know one another more or less; all share in the same amusements, are interested in the same topics, and arrange their lives more or less according to the same scheme. No doubt the Anglo-Indian would dispute this, and point out countless differences; but it is indisputably true that this is the impression on the stranger.

It inevitably follows that in such a society, composed of those engaged in serious work, highly trained, and of education far above any general average at home, the tone both of manners and of intelligence is high. Similarity there may be; but it is similarity with a very high common standard. One symptom is born of the habit of constant contact with a subject race. It is that of what may be called a certain circumspection of demeanour. One notices varieties of manner in the treatment of the native, and occasionally a rough or supercilious element obtrudes itself rather harshly. A young subaltern now and then, in his first year of India, in pure ignorance, treats an Indian of position with the callow discourtesy of a schoolboy. It is an error which he soon learns to drop, but which often works evil out of proportion to any ill intention. More harm still is done by the rough manners, natural to his kind, of the low-class Englishman. But, as a rule, the educated Anglo-Indian has learned, under severe provocation, to hold himself severely in check. He knows what *prestige* means to him, and his life is one long education in the adjustment of his attitude towards those whose natural bent is often to an undue servility, mixed with a self-evident dissimulation. For his own welfare and theirs, he knows that he must not derogate from his position, and this almost unconsciously develops the circumspectness, without the pride, of an aristocratic bearing. Without it, our rule in India would not last a year; and the lack of dignity that shows itself in supercilious arrogance or cheap familiarity has no more stern critic than the high-class Anglo-Indian official—and he is, of course, the dominant element in this society. There is no more ludicrous mistake than to see in it a selfish desire to exploit India for their own good. Lahore is not even, so far as the native is concerned, a wealthy place; but there is at least one native who could easily buy up the whole English community. In Delhi there are probably hundreds who could do so. No Anglo-Indian here is a capitalist. None of them owns an acre of land. Neither money nor landed influence gives them one jot of their power. They hold their place solely by the power of a proud bearing which has no tincture of superciliousness, of earnest and unselfish work, and of absolute justice, which, in their hearts, all the different sections of those whom they rule are compelled to acknowledge.

There are other features which strike a stranger with a certain sadness. Increase of necessary expenses—the rapid rise of prices—these have brought new cares and anxieties to the heavy burden of Indian official life. A generation ago the scale of official pay here recompensed those who undertook the life, with all its drawbacks, by an income which was considerable in comparison with the average professional prospects at home. This is no longer the same; and yet the drawbacks are there in all their force. Behind all the happy *camaraderie*, one sees the shadows that tell us why this is "the land of regrets." There are the forced partings and the long absence from children, for whom, after a time, the climate and the surroundings are unsuitable. There is the constant dread of the coming of the hot season, when households must perforce be broken up, and wives and nurseries must fly to the hills, leaving the bread-winner to swelter in the plains. Just now the weather is cool, and the mornings and evenings chilly. One notes the pleasure with which fires are kindled, greatcoats are donned, and the habits of English life adopted with something of a jesting protest. They really hug the cold, and their complaints of it are little but a joke. Just at this moment the prospect of happy meetings and a bright time at Christmas sends a cheerful influence over all. But the cloud of the warm weather casts its shadow before it, and it forms the real grimness of their lives. Yet it does not check their zest in the work and the amusement of life. They are busy from morning to night. They are out early for a ride in the fresh coolness of the morning. They are at work at an hour that would be early for professional work in London. As soon as office hours are over, they gather in the garden of their friends or of the Montgomery

Hall, in a crowd that comprises practically the whole throng of Anglo-Indians, for active exercise. Judges and high officials, military officers and ladies, all alike keep *ennui* away by habits of exercise that would put our professional men at home to shame. The cheerfulness that is born of a strenuous life is indubitably theirs. The listless native watches it all with apathetic astonishment, not unmixed with admiration. The centre of the whole is in Government House, which, with its fair gardens and well-timbered lawns, lies close by the Lawrence Gardens and the spacious club buildings. From that centre all the life and work of the city radiates. Its gracious hospitality and its ever-present sympathy send out a glow of good-will that permeates everywhere. He would be dull of perception who did not perceive the unstinted loyalty of the whole band of officials towards the chief who guides the destiny of some twenty million souls, or does not recognise the admiration which indomitable courage and energy, that no ill-health can daunt, call forth from his subordinates.[1]

[1] Since this was written, the well-loved Lieut.-Governor of

Another aspect of life is that of the British officers of Indian regiments, of which there is a goodly company five miles off at Mianmir. Lahore sometimes goes to them; they, still more often, come to Lahore, thinking little of these five miles of supremely dusty roads. We have had more than one display of the marvellous horsemanship of these officers and their troops. In all the regular exercises of tent-pegging and the rest the officers more than hold their own against these hardy Pathan horsemen, to whom a horse seems like a part of themselves. It is only in the dexterities of trick riding—standing upright on the saddle at full gallop, or firing a revolver and picking up a handkerchief while lying backwards across the saddle—that the dignity of the officer forbids his participation, though it was whispered that it was not due to lack of proved capacity for the exploits. They win the hearts and the respect of their men by sharing in all their sport and by the brotherhood of mastery in their art.

It is pleasant, too, to watch their pride in

the Punjab, Sir Denzil Ibbetson, has succumbed to his disease and ended his heroic fight.

the splendid efficiency of their corps, and their ardent confidence in its loyalty—not the less real that they are alive to the fact that dangerous elements may not always be visible, even to the eye of close and constant observers. That danger they are ready to face, although they fully recognise how deceptive were appearances in pre-Mutiny days. Knowing, as they do, the insidious attempts that are made to undermine loyalty, is it wonderful that they resent any encouragement that such attempts may receive from the recklessness of superficial observers, who come from home with a preconceived prejudice against all authority, and an ineradicable conviction that those who wield it must always be in the wrong? They are a strong prop of our Indian Empire, and may have to face grim danger for her sake; but now it is a pleasure to see their cheery, yet wary, confidence, their thorough absorption in their work, and the cordiality of their relations with the native officers and men—all of whom come from a self-respecting class of yeomen, who would scorn any menial work.

XI

RELATIONS BETWEEN NATIVES AND ANGLO-INDIANS

LAHORE, *December* 16, 1907.

IN my last letter I spoke of some of the aspects of Anglo-Indian life which strike the visitor after some weeks of observation. There are, of course, other matters which press upon the attention. But here, even if ordinary caution did not prevent dogmatism, a moderate sense of humour, not unmixed with fear of the natural sarcasm with which the experience of long years regards the confidence of the outsider, would preserve any man from rash expression of opinion. Long interest in, and study of, Indian questions, and such knowledge as comes from constant correspondence over a long series of years, only justifies a very tentative estimate of some of the problems that present themselves. New developments do not abate, but rather increase their difficulty.

Take as an example one curious institution —deeply rooted in native prejudice, productive of the maximum of inconvenience, and capable of defence by no one—that of the *octroi* or city dues which are everywhere prevalent. A city like this cannot be maintained without a revenue, and a house tax or rate would arouse against it the whole weight of native prejudice. The *octroi* is the only alternative; and it is productive of such inconvenience as nothing but the boundlessness of Oriental patience could endure. At the various entrances to Lahore we find a long string of carts, waiting for hours for their pass and for the settlement of the dues. The native is blissfully ignorant of the fact that this clumsy method increases the cost of his life, and brings a maximum of friction into his trade. It gives ample opportunity for the petty tyranny and exactions of the lower native official. Official intelligence universally condemns it. Its evils are patent to any one who looks at it rationally. But it is buttressed by a prejudice which only patient contrivance can hope to overcome. It would be well if the educated natives devoted some of their energies to exposing its absurdity, and so paving the way for the adoption of a substitute.

One phase of Anglo-Indian life cannot fail to strike an outsider. In the sense in which it exists amongst us at home for good or ill the Press and its influence are practically *nil.* The Anglo-Indian glances at the *Pioneer* or the *Civil and Military Gazette.* About a quarter or less of each paper is given to telegrams and articles; the rest is advertisements. The European telegrams are of the scantiest—about as long as Reuter's sheet on the notice-board of a club. For the rest, the articles—it may be excellent in their way—are often on subjects of merely general interest, which might appear next week or next month as well as to-day. Two or three minutes suffice for the perusal of the paper to the average Anglo-Indian, and I have not in any club met with a copy of that essential of life to the ordinary Englishman at home—the great daily British newspaper. I fear our ordinary topics are of minor interest here. The native papers, apart from those in the vernacular, are the *Punjabi*—of which the less said the better—and the *Tribune*. The latter is the organ of the moderate Hindu party. I can only judge it by what I have myself seen; and I am bound to say that I have not read a word which is open to objection. We may not share all its views. But it is a model of fair and reasonable comment, and no sedition, nothing tending to encourage resistance to authority or to foster insane ambitions, has appeared in any number of the paper that I have seen.[1]

I touch upon more delicate ground, and one on which a new-comer must be specially wary of undue confidence, when I speak of the relations between the native and the Anglo-Indian society. In the background lie the larger political questions; but these are powerfully affected by what shows upon the surface—the social difficulty. It is the aspect of the matter which irresistibly affects the views of all. One must remember the peculiar

[1] I regret to say that since this was written the *Tribune* has fallen into worse hands.

conditions which give to it its prominence. At home it would not, I suppose, be an easy thing for any of us—even if he took the trouble to think of it—to know what his own social position is. The *strata* of society are considerably mixed, and I fancy most of us take our place as circumstances decide it for us, and are satisfied with our surroundings without troubling to classify ourselves or others. But here it is different. The line of social demarcation, in a community like this, is of necessity clearly marked, and the instinct of self-preservation gives it strength. That there is a cleavage between the European and the Native is indubitable; and much as the best amongst both concur in desiring to lessen it, its complete disappearance is impossible, and clumsy efforts to efface it are productive of much more harm than good. It depends largely upon what may appear to be paltry, but are very real, hindrances to constant intercourse. In the petty details of personal habits, the customs of the native are sometimes as disagreeable to us as ours probably are to him. The native gentleman looks upon the use of a pocket-handkerchief with as much disgust as we do upon habits which dispense with it. The use of a hand-basin is to him something which savours of uncleanliness. It is useless to multiply instances; it is enough to say that they are a substantial bar to pleasant social intercourse. But there are more serious matters. To the Hindu of conservative views and rigid etiquette it is positively distasteful to meet a woman in social life, and both the Hindu and the Mussulman, from the necessity of segregating their female relations, must enter society not only with a perpetual difference in their relations to it, but with a perpetually implied condemnation of—or rather contempt for—our usages. Can social intercourse be easy on either side under these conditions? Add to this that the Hindu cannot eat with us without infringing his most cherished feelings; and this acts as a bar to that large part of social intercourse which depends upon hospitality. In this respect the Hindu is equally divided from the Mohammedan.

The difficulties are not to be met by any rough-and-ready solution, of the kind which may be suggested very largely perhaps by those whose perception of social relations are not the most keen. I can only say that I have spoken to many native gentlemen, from the octogenarian representative of an old family with aristocratic traditions, and more keenly interested in reminiscences of Chillianwallah than in controversies of the present day, down to the youngest barrister or pleader, fresh from his years in London and his dinners at an Inn of Court, or from his B.A. examination at the University, and I have found them all, in proportion to their power of judgment, impressed with the difficulty of the problem. In several cases I found them not only ready to enter into, but to initiate, discussion of the subject. This is in itself instructive. We do not intermingle political questions with drawing-room etiquette, and feel surprised when a man rates himself according to the invitations he receives. But the native is sensitive on such points, and perhaps those natives are most sensitive who feel that educational advantages on which they pride themselves do not secure for them that respect and position amongst their own nationality to which they think they are entitled.

Frankly, the young educated native—or the product of that which is alone counted as education in India, that is to say a course of English literature, modern philosophy, and constitutional history—does not seem to me to compare favourably with his elders. He has learned to attire himself in European dress of such sartorial perfection as to be a caricature. He has learned expensive habits, which are strange to his father. He has assumed a deeper semblance of servility in manner, with an additional ply of dissimulation, which displays itself at every turn. His political aspirations do not appear to be very comprehensive or to extend much beyond his own class. He likes the elective principle, because his powers of speech and his readiness of device will help him to win the prizes in that race. Political freedom means to him an increase in the number of Government posts to which he can aspire. Constitutional privilege is the power to draw Government pay and to secure the consideration which official position gives.

Of course, this does not represent the whole, but judging from those I have seen, it applies not unfairly to a considerable proportion of the class. I have also met older men of assured position, and with less of personal ambition, who belonged to the Arya Somaj and spoke to me readily of its aims. They describe it as a society having for its aim to preserve the sanctity and authority of the Hindu scriptures, while modifying the principle of caste, so as to make it depend less upon birth and more upon individual character. There have been similar attempts before; but they said that the failure of at least one such attempt in recent times was due to its undermining the authority of the scriptures, or, as we might say, because its latitudinarianism went a little too far. It is easy to see how the doctrine they profess offers attractions to a class which conceives itself unjustly looked down upon by the older aristocracy of their own race, although one detects something amiss in a religion which seeks to decide, according to its own dictates, the several grades of society upon a criterion applied to each individual.

All of them declared the religious element to stand first in the doctrine of the Somaj. Some of them frankly admitted that it had at the same time a political aim; and that aim is always ascribed to it by those natives who are opposed to the association, and sometimes very bitterly opposed to it on that very ground. Those whom I have spoken to were all men who had earned general respect, and who did not belong to the extreme party—although, perhaps, the expression of extreme opinions has recently been somewhat restrained. The political aim towards which all those who admittedly favoured change are inclined is the extension of representative institutions; and the apparent unfitness of the ordinary zemindar for such institutions seemed to them to be no valid objection to their adoption. An education which tends to theory much more than practice may be partly the cause of this, but I fancy it would hardly be denied that it owes something to the desire to break down the traditional aristocratic impulse and to diminish the authority of the British official.

Those who actually exercise that authority

are naturally averse to pronouncing an opinion, where there is so much to watch and so much need of caution. But their position seems to me to be comparable to nothing so much as that of scientific engineers planning, with elaborate and careful foresight, out of the most heterogeneous materials, a vast work, and suddenly called upon to entrust its guidance to the irresponsible votes of the navvies engaged upon the manual labour of construction. The dangers involved are to them too patent to be lightly dismissed, and they are so familiar with them, and with the complexity of this problem, that they hardly think it needful to expound them. It was plainly asserted to me that the class which chiefly pressed for change were closely connected with the Banyah, or money-lending class, whose desire for land-ownership has received a severe check from the Land Alienation Act, restricting the alienation of mortgaged lands. In revenge for this, and to secure additional support for their propaganda, it was asserted that they had fostered discontent amongst the zemindars in the Canal Colonies, who are irritated by the economic rules laid down for the management of their lands, the real necessity of which they do not comprehend. I can, of course, offer no opinion as to this; I only state a current belief, for which apparently strong ground was shown. This much I can state with certainty, that I have nowhere heard more bitter denunciation of the new proposals than I heard from many of the older-fashioned Hindus and Sikhs, and from almost every Mohammedan with whom I have spoken. No member of the Somaj failed to disown for himself any desire to bring British authority to an end, or to recognise such a possibility as fraught with danger to the country. "No one can dread such a result more than ourselves," said one of them with considerable frankness, "because we are not a fighting race and would be at the mercy of other more violent races." One seems to detect in this rather too much of an echo of British opinion to accept it as entirely spontaneous. However that may be, there can be no doubt that the natives who are opposed to the new aspirations, ascribe to them that as their ultimate aim, and regard a rash adoption of Western Constitutional ideas, so radically opposed to the traditional instincts of the East, as certain either to lead to that end, or to plunge the country into the most bitter strife. We must not imagine that loyalty such as that of the Rajputs is a mere passive quality. They hold it deep in their hearts because they believe it to be the best defence of their cherished traditions, and anything that would break these traditions would not only starve their loyalty, but would kindle their active opposition. We cannot play with fireworks over a powder magazine.

This much is certain, that the wisest and the most moderate men, both amongst Anglo-Indian officials and amongst native gentlemen of position, are impressed with the conviction that a ferment has been excited, and artificially excited, in India. Whether it has spent its force or not, remains to be seen; and also whether the moderate reforming party has dissociated itself from the extremists. For the moment the latter have lost credit. It remains to be seen whether they have been effectively warned. No outsider can reasonably pronounce an opinion. I can only say that the strongest views I have heard as to the existence of a danger have been expressed to me by natives of India; nor can we be surprised that they regard with misgiving any extension of the power of the subordinate native official, who is often the curse of the country, and whose misdoings, especially in the public works and the railway department, I have heard bitterly denounced by natives. For the rest, we must be content to learn and weigh the views of those whose experience is most ripe, and in whose rigid justice we may feel confident. It is to be hoped that due caution will prevail at Westminster, where, after all, the key of India lies.

XII

A VISIT TO A NATIVE STATE

AGRA, *December* 21, 1907.

I HAD good reason to find it something of a wrench to say good-bye to Lahore. It has left none but good impressions, although I would have wished that the grip of the drought had lifted, if only for an hour or two, before I saw the last of Lahore, and had allowed me to see it otherwise than under the heavy pall of dust that has been accumulating since August, and has shorn it of much of its usual beauty. The capital of the Punjab must remain to me as the chief type of Anglo-Indian life, outside the three great cities; and whatever the advantages or dis-advantages, or the peculiar idiosyncrasies, of the places that I have seen, or may see, it will, I suppose, be accepted as a fair specimen of its class. I passed after it into a very different scene.

Bad as the drought is everywhere, one is less struck with it on the journey from Lahore eastwards to Rajpura than elsewhere —say, round Delhi, where the eye can range over a boundless extent of arid plain, made sadder still by signs that the ground has been ploughed, although to no purpose. There are here many green patches and wide fields of apparently good sugar-cane. Canal irrigation has done much in this region to mitigate the evil—although it may well be that compared with an average year the deficit is here as great as elsewhere. As we approach the railway junction of Rajpura the woodland becomes thicker than I have yet seen it, and in the evening light it looks as if we were passing into a region of almost boundless wooded country. This remains the aspect of the landscape as we approach Patiala.

This was my first experience of a native State; and it was full of interest. The State has a population of about a million and a half, composed of Hindus, Sikhs, and Mohammedans, and the ruling family is Sikh.

It belongs to a little contiguous group of native States, called the Phulkian States, which are associated together by having one British Resident, representing the Imperial authority to them all. The chief town of the Patiala State is that from which it takes its name, and has a population of some sixty thousand. It has the appearance of a thriving town, and its open streets, generally broad and fairly clean, and well built, compare favourably with some of the narrower and grubbier thoroughfares that I have seen elsewhere. It has some handsome buildings—notably a hospital, a school, and an imposing College, and a very fine set of State offices has just been erected. The Fort is a fine specimen of Sikh architecture, and besides serving as a citadel and as a receptacle for the Maharajah's treasures, is the residence of the ladies who formed the zenana of the late Maharajah. From its portals these ladies never emerge. The revenue, including the Maharajah's Civil List, is about £700,000; and, out of that, whatever dilapidations it suffered a few years back, a sufficient fund is formed, not only for the maintenance of a splendid Imperial Service Force of some 2500 cavalry and infantry, but also for careful sanitary and engineering work, and for the support of several thriving educational establishments.

But it is not on these aspects of this independent native State that I would lay emphasis, but rather on the picturesque phase of life that it presents. No stranger can enter the State except as the guest of the Maharajah or his representatives. The present Maharajah is a handsome youth of about sixteen years of age, whom I met as a pupil of the Chiefs' College at Lahore; and the power is exercised by a Council of Regency, consisting generally of three persons—a Hindu, a Sikh, and a Mohammedan—although the death of the Hindu, a short time before my visit, had caused a vacancy in the number. The hospitality of the State is exercised in a fine Guest House, called the *Moti Bagh*, or Pearl Garden, which stands in a splendid park of its own, and nothing is spared in the way of graceful courtesy and of stately profusion to maintain the dignity of the Maharajah. Guards are placed beside all the portals.

There is a crowd of well-trained servants in the State livery of green and gold, with the arms of the Maharajah's house emblazoned on their coats. The members of the Council vie with one another in maintaining all the punctilio of a dignified courtesy, which it would be hard to parallel anywhere but in the East. The wishes of the guest are consulted at each step, and nothing is omitted to make him feel that he is enjoying a hospitality carefully adjusted to European habits.

Wide though the differences of view may be between the representatives of the different religions, they are at one in being most cordial friends of English rule. Whatever may be the case elsewhere, there is no unrest here, if it be not the unrest of alarm about incautious change. Nowhere have I found native gentlemen with more of interest in the British administration than here in this independent State. They had studied the leading phases of party politics at home, and understood the influence of the Press. They recognised the changes that had been brought about in the last generation, and saw that the government of India worked under a much fiercer light of criticism than in past days. Although quite conscious that popular reforms would not affect their own State, they deprecated their incautious adoption as likely to lead to serious difficulties between the different races of India. If there was an Arya Somaj Association, there was also, it was explained to me, the *Sanatamdhurm*—the name adopted by those who are opposed to the innovations of the Somaj. No later than in April of this year, there was established an *Anjuman*, or Association of the Rajputs of all India, and its first conference was held at Patiala. Probably the Mohammedan influence was the most active in organising the conference, but they form only a small proportion of the Rajputs. The number of Rajputs all over India is nearly ten millions, of whom nearly seven millions are Hindus, nearly two millions are Mohammedans, and the remainder of various religions. They are of all degrees of wealth; but a vast proportion of them, in spite of their pride of birth and pure descent, are amongst the poorest peasantry. The primary objects of the conference were to promote the economical welfare, and to improve the education of the Rajputs; but resolutions were passed by the conference strongly urging the necessity of loyalty to British rule, as prescribed by the principles of their race. No doubt the Mohammedan element was most prominent in the conference; but it was joined by many Hindus and many Sikhs, and was held under the patronage of the Council of Regency, in which there is only one Mohammedan member.

The aims of the conference, the proceedings of which have been published, were explained to me very fully by Colonel Abdul Majid Khan, the Foreign Minister of Patiala, who took an active part in its organisation. He has recently contributed to the Press some interesting letters on the teaching of the Koran with respect to friendship to Christians, which he regards as inculcated by the precepts of his religion, and he holds that agitation against the ruling power in India is not only dangerous as regards its probable results, but distinctly contrary to his faith. It would be absurd for me to express an opinion on a doctrinal point of so much difficulty, and I must equally refrain from estimating all the motives that may have been operative in such a conference. But it is none the less noteworthy that both by Hindu and Mohammedan gentlemen, of high culture, and not likely to under-estimate the advantages of education, strong opinions were expressed to me that the neglect of distinctive religious teaching for the various communities — the subject being pushed aside by the fever about competitive examinations—was undermining the best part of the national character of all the races, and was in great measure responsible for an agitation which they alleged to be engineered by a small and not highly-respected class. I confess the secondary place of religious teaching in the schools was one of the features of our educational system in India that had already suggested doubts in my own mind, and I know that such doubts are shared by experienced Anglo-Indian officials. At Patiala, for instance, I saw a girls' school, recently established on English lines, which would seem to be an experiment requiring very delicate handling. The buildings were handsome, but the attendance is as yet small; and although it is both for Hindu and Mohammedan girls, and seemed to be well conducted, I fancied that the Mohammedan gentleman who accompanied me to the school felt that very prudent management was necessary. He did not himself visit the schoolrooms, and I was rather surprised to find sitting in one of the younger classes a girl of thirteen, who was already living in wedlock. The semblance of educational activity is not everything, and a Western example, followed with undue zeal, may sometimes travesty its model. It is a hazardous thing lightly to set aside ancestral habits, based upon religious belief. I leave it to others with more experience to say whether we are careful enough to avoid undermining such habits without putting anything in their place. It is not, I should fancy, from the pleader class, with their humbler birth and their lack of consideration amongst the inarticulate mass of their fellow-nationalists, and basing their ambition upon a University degree, that the most effective warning against such dangers is likely to come.

But, after all, leaving graver questions aside

for the moment, it is in the open-air life of Patiala that its chief charm lies. Whatever regrets there may be at the waste of splendid material in the prematurely-ended career of the late Maharajah, there can be no doubt that he has powerfully impressed upon his people an ardent love of sport and of all the essentials of a manly life. A magnificent sportsman himself, absolutely incapable of fear, much of the failure of his life was due to an excess of kindliness. But it cannot be said that he lived in vain. The revenues of his State were impaired, but wise tutelage may do much to amend that. Meanwhile the essentials of good administration are not stinted, and one has only to see the splendid troops which are provided for the Imperial service, the unsurpassed horsemanship, and the pervading pluck and courage in all athletic contests, to be convinced that his example has given manliness in a supreme degree to his little nation. I saw parades of their cavalry and infantry—many of their soldiers wearing the medal of the Tirah campaign, where the late Maharajah served us well; and there, as well as on the polo ground, in their wrestling and their gymnastic exercises —not forgetting the quoit-throwing in which they showed their skill with what was an old Sikh weapon of war—an activity and keenness were shown, not soon to pass from one's memory. It is not surprising that the officers of our own cavalry regiments are apt to regard these Imperial Service troops with something of friendly jealousy.

It was with regret that I paid my visit of adieu to the Council of Regency. I was received in the handsome durbar room of the new public offices, which by chance was then used for the first time. I was presented with the *atta* and *pan*—scent and sweetmeat—which is the mark of native courtesy, and the usual formality of laying gifts before the guest was duly carried out. I had seen much of what was of special and peculiar interest as a new phase of Indian life; and had conversations which made one fully appreciate the intelligence and wide knowledge of my hosts, however little I could form any authoritative opinion on the grave topics which they discussed so freely, except to estimate their difficulty and the urgent need of caution, where the different motives, aims, and currents of thought are woven into a tangle so complicated. I may give one curious illustration of this. In a conversation with some of the Ministers of the State, a view adverse to irrigation on the ground that it tended to diminish the physical fitness of the inhabitants, was quoted with some expression of surprise. But I found that the view was not only shared, but defended with plausible arguments, by my friends. Irrigation, they said, by involving double crops, kept the population incessantly at agricultural labour, which diminished their fighting power. In older days they lived more simply; trusted only to the rain, and cultivated more intermittently; and had, therefore, more leisure for high physical development and the gaining of military prowess. They had no thought of stinting expenditure on irrigation; and, in spite of what they deemed to be its drawbacks, they were prepared to face as inevitable a total change in the agricultural economics of the country. Their opinion might be right or wrong; but prejudice in favour of tradition was not at least allowed to determine their action.

It was at Patiala Station, I think, that a curious incident related to me occurred. A British officer was discussing with a Mohammedan friend of high rank the political situation. "Tell me," he said, "do you believe that, in the days of my grandsons and yours, India will still be under British rule?" They happened to be standing close to the water-tank, with its usual inscriptions at each end, "Water for Mohammedan gentlemen," "Water for Hindu gentlemen." The native gentleman pointed to it, and said, "So long as that remains you must be here."

XIII

THE GLORIES OF AGRA

LUCKNOW, *December* 21, 1907.

FROM Patiala I travelled to Agra, by Delhi, where I spent another night. Each new visit to a place teaches us more of it, and I was glad for a third time to see its vast stretches of crumbling tombs, the towering heights of its Jumma Masjid, and the long red walls of the Fort, with the untidy masses of ill-stored wealth, and the oddly jumbled crowd of all nationalities—so strangely contrasting with the old-world quiet and restfulness of the native State. I reached Agra in the full heat of the afternoon, and the long drive from the junction station, past crumbling shanties and parched fields, did not afford any very inviting view. It is only when you come into the English civil lines that the characteristic aspects of the place begin to show themselves. There are none of the long, shady avenues, with tall, overhanging trees, that one sees at Peshawar and Lahore. The bungalows do not hide themselves behind thick hedges which show only occasional glimpses of garden and verandah. On the contrary, the trees are smaller and sparser, and in place of the hedges there are endless lines of stucco balustrade. There are wide stretches of level lawns, which ought now to be green and flourishing, but which the long drought has left parched and yellow. The bungalows have no longer the usual flat roofs, with the tall projection in the centre, but have generally sloping roofs of thatch, which promise coolness and protection from the sun in the warm season.

The difference of aspect is something; but you have not been long in Agra before seeing that you are in a new province and under a new régime. The contrast between the different provinces is greater than a new-comer is prepared for. The very policeman, with his khaki uniform and close-fitting red puggaree, is in sharp contrast with the blue tunic and big turban of his brother in the Punjab, and one imagines, perhaps wrongly, that his manner varies in accordance with the different population with which he has to deal. One hears no longer the familiar names of the big officials of the Punjab; new names are in every mouth. The land laws are, in important respects, different; and instead of a multitude of small owners, the larger landlord is here a power in the land. One hears little here about unrest, and rumours of sedition are said to be at a discount. The Sikh no longer makes his presence felt, and the Mohammedan seems more frequently to wear his distinctive fez. The British soldier is more in evidence than he was at Lahore, and the long lines of his trim cantonments, with all the order and cleanliness of a barrack square at home, stretch away at no great distance along the straight, dusty roads, so different from the winding, tree-bordered avenues of Lahore. You see all this, and notice distinctions in the current talk and topics of those whom you meet, long before you have passed to the great glories of Agra—its Fort and its wondrous Taj. I would almost be inclined to say that the difference in passing from one province of British India to another strikes the new-comer more than any difference to be found in passing from the Orange River Colony to the Transvaal. In one point, however, they are all alike—the constant, quiet activity of official work. I had not been long in Agra before I saw, as a piece of everyday routine before his office work began, the inspection by a young civilian of a crowd of applicants for poor relief. The family history, the ordinary employment, the sources of livelihood of each applicant, were carefully examined, and no case was decided without the physical condition and the clothing of each being inspected. There were curious hindrances to the work. Many applicants did not turn up for inspection, because they dreaded that compulsory inoculation for the plague would be a part of the proceedings. Others unblushingly stated that, although they wanted relief, they were "too respectable" to work; others openly avowed themselves professional beggars; while signs of clever acting were not wanting in other cases. Each case was judged with the usual patience and the usual prompt impartiality.

A drive of a mile or more along these broad dusty roads, with their border of sparse trees and white balustrades, brings you to the Fort of Akbar, and you are once more, as at Delhi, amongst the memorials of the Mogul Empire. In most ways this Fort at Agra is far more impressive than that at Delhi. The towering wall is bigger and more imposing, and within, instead of a vast space, over which the splendid remnants of their sumptuous buildings are sprinkled as mere specks upon the arena, you have a great pile of closely connected buildings, representing every phase of Mogul art. The paved road leads us up gradually to the summit, through buildings of very varying character. We pass through the great portals of Akbar's palace, with its grimmer and sterner architecture in red stone, and its ever-present reminiscences of Hindu types, and its carved figures of animals, so out of harmony with Mogul art. At length we come to the lovely Moti Masjid, or Pearl Mosque, far larger than that at Delhi, and with its white domes and minarets shining bright in the sun at the summit of the ascent. To my mind, with its perfect purity of white and its delicate carving, so free from all meretricious ornament, it is even more entrancing than the more gorgeous Diwani and the small and almost toy-like Pearl Mosque of Delhi Fort; and in situation it is incomparably finer. There is here a mixture of religious edifice with the grim strength of a huge fortification, and with all the strange medley of a palace, every chamber of which can be appropriated accurately to its use, that gives to the whole an interest which has no parallel at Delhi. There are special associations attached to the marvellously beautiful living apartment, where Shahjahan's wife—the *Muntaz-i-Mahl*, or "Jewel of the Palace"—passed her days, and where her husband, in his old age, six-and-thirty years after her death, spent his latest days, with Jahanara, the only daughter, who kept her love for him faithfully till his death. He was then shorn of all his splendour and his luxury, the captive of his own son, Aurungzebe; and the consolation of these last years of his life was found in gazing from the balconies upon the wondrous tomb, lying full in view beyond a bend in the

Jumna, which he had raised in memory of the wife of his youth. His daughter exchanged her office of tender companion for a religious life, and lies buried in the humble grass-covered grave beside the tomb of the Saint Nizamuddin, near Delhi. Little as we can share the thoughts of the race, and lightly as we may hold the annals of their luxury, their splendours, their pomp, and their cruelties, we cannot but be touched by the picture of vain regrets and of filial love. *Mentem mortalia tangunt.*

We pass beyond the Fort, and drive for another mile or two across a wide-spreading and well-ordered park, which relieves the eye accustomed to monotonous plains by its graceful undulations and its wooded dells; and slowly the miracle of Agra, the Taj, opens on our view—at first a white dome, encircled by dazzling minarets, and then slowly showing its surroundings of portal and mosque, contrasting with its snowy brilliancy and simplicity in their deep warm red, and in the fantastic and rich ornamentation of their façades and parapets. The Taj rises above them, vast and majestic, in its perfect simplicity of outline, solid, and yet seeming at times almost to melt into cloud and sky. We pass through two courtyards of red stone, bordered with *serais*, and on through its richly decorated portal of red, chequered with variegated marbles, into the long peaceful garden with its rows of Italian cypresses, its trim flower beds, its marble paths, and its pools and fountains, at the far end of which rises, above marble staircase and platform, the vast mass of pure white outlining itself against the deep blue of the sky. All doubts, all fears of disappointed expectations, all feelings except that of over-mastering beauty, are swept away; and each step, as we come nearer to it, and it gradually dwarfs the foliage that lies below, confirms the magic of its unrivalled grace. By this alone, one is tempted to think, the voyage to India would be repaid.

All the world knows something of the Taj, and it is no business of mine to attempt to criticise it, or to enter upon any architectural discussion of its merits or demerits. No one knows for certain its architect; and doubts are entertained as to the sources of inspiration which were drawn upon in its creation. For us it is linked with none of those associations of Western architectural treasures, the work of men who were bone of our bone, and by whose lives and thoughts our own lives and thoughts have been shaped and moulded, and out of whom we have grown. We only know it as the legacy of men whose pomp and triumphs, whose ambitions and struggles, whose luxury and cruelties, are something alien from all our history, and belong to another world than ours. On the forced labour and the long-drawn miseries of countless thousands, this marvellous creation was growing, just when our Long Parliament was wrangling, and when Cavalier and Roundhead were struggling with one another; and its author died when Charles II. was in the early zenith of his reign, and in the year when St. Paul's and half of London were destroyed by fire. They were far from us in idea and in purpose, but yet the thought often occurs how short is our historical retrospect over this land of remote antiquity. At the Kutab and Tuglukabad we are carried back to the days of our Plantagenets; but for the most part, throughout the scenes amongst which I have passed, one hardly ever recalls history more distant than the days of Milton. We are apt to forget that Milton and Dryden drew their images of Eastern pomp from no ancient annals, and no fabulous chroniclers, but from the freshest stories of travellers and ambassadors of their own day, whose accounts were current in the mouths of men, and told them of a strange world so unlike their own.

I have no architectural criticism to offer; and just as little can I idealise the Taj by any theory of fanciful symbolism. The story of Shahjahan, with all his easy bonhomie, his laxity of creed, his life of mingled fighting and debauchery, blended with his passionate and enduring love for the wife of his youth, and the sadness of his closing years, must always have an interest of its own. But in this creation of surpassing beauty I can find nothing that reflects the sadness of human fate, or that tells of the all-pervading solemnity of death. There is nothing of sad or mournful reminiscence, nothing of the infinite regret for love that is only a memory. It tells of no grief for the immutable decrees of fate; it is a defiance of death by associating it with all the bright and gossamer gleam of sunlight and of fairy beauty. It stands supremely alone, not by the power of any pathos, or of any appeal to the sympathy which the woes of humanity evoke, but as the brightest, the most joyous, the most luxuriant monument of death and decay that the world has ever seen. We are spell-bound by its surpassing beauty; but we feel that the world of thought and feeling that went to its creation was a different world from our own. That beauty sinks the deeper the longer we linger by it; it is increased by each visit; it is enhanced by every sight of it—in the hazy mists of the morning, in the blaze of the mid-day sun, when the evening shades are lengthening, and, more perhaps than all, in the cold silvery light of the moon under a sky of deepest blue. But after all, it is still to the eye, and not to the heart, that it appeals. The "Jewel of the Palace" was enshrined in a casket that reflected all the trappings of joy and luxury, and that bore no traces of the mystery and sadness of regret, and death, and parting hearts. Sorrow, for us, seeks another garb; but the world could ill spare this one joyous and miraculously graceful transfiguration of the mournfulness of human fate.

XIV

LAND NATIONALISATION—A GARDEN OF BLOOD.

ALLAHABAD, *December* 28, 1907.

IT helps one to understand the complexity of Indian questions and to see how different currents are perpetually crossing one another, when one watches the changes that show themselves as we pass from one province to another. The same influences work in entirely different ways owing to new conditions, and one ceases to be surprised at the various different currents of opinion amongst leading officials. They are due to no spirit of wrangling or opposition, but largely to the varying problems which they have to meet.

In the United Provinces, for instance, we are told that there is less of "unrest" than in the Punjab. But along with this, in Oudh at least, there is a considerable amount of violence and crime, and robbery and even murder are not rare. Why is it that this is not accompanied by incentives to political turbulence? In manufacturing districts like Cawnpore the field might seem to be open to its instigators; the poverty seems to be there greater than in the Punjab, while the barren tracts between Cawnpore and Lucknow seem to show an even greater danger of famine than in the neighbouring province. It may be that the lesson of the Mutiny is here more fresh in the memory of men. The fusion of different provinces may have rendered a common understanding amongst mischiefmongers more difficult. A stronger infusion of the Anglo-Indian element, and the presence of larger military cantonments, may tell the same way. But beyond and above all these there can be no doubt that the influence of the larger land-holders, their general loyalty, and the sympathy that has of late years been shown to their traditions, which has enhanced that loyalty, have been powerful agents in promoting political security. Only fifteen months intervened between the annexation of Oudh and the Mutiny, and there can be little doubt that the drastic interference with the old order of things did much to stimulate the rebellious instinct. Of late years more sympathy has been shown to that traditionary influence which rightly belongs to the older families, and which forms, especially to the Oriental mind, so powerful a solvent of political unrest. It is a strange comment upon rash attempts to introduce Western notions, destructive of the rights of property, into a soil like this, that the basis of land tenure in India is undoubtedly Socialistic, and that there exists here a real nationalisation of land. But an administration based on land nationalisation does well to recognise that for the public good it is unwise to introduce distrust and anarchy by riding roughshod over inherited notions and over that deep-rooted respect for old-established rights of which the Oriental is so tenacious. That such tendencies may be based on an honest desire to obey abstract principles of popular right will not make the result less dangerous. Many of our wisest Anglo-Indian administrators hold that the legitimate influence of the hereditary families, and the ready acquiescence in that influence of the mass of this enormous population of fifty millions, forms an important foundation and buttress of settled order in the United Provinces. I can speak only of what I have learned from those best able to judge, but there can be no doubt of the general trend of opinion in that direction. We cannot administer India on a set of abstract principles, wielded by a bureaucracy. We must attach weight to the political and social and economical history of the country. Deprive the older families of their legitimate influence, and you will then make them the rooted enemies of all modern movements, filled with contempt for upstarts—as they deem them—who have got a veneer of education; and these upstarts, in their turn, will use agitation as a ready means of self-advertisement, and of pressing their own influence against that of the native aristocracy, and at the same time against British rule. You will be driven, perforce, to depend more and more upon the subordinate native officials, who are the direst oppressors of their own countrymen, and, except under constant supervision, the most dangerous agents of your own rule. Give to that native aristocracy their hereditary influence and their just rights, and you will have a class through whom you can maintain your hold upon the vast inarticulate mass of native zemindars, who will be the medium between the bureaucratic administration and the people, and with whom the new educated class will find it their interest to coalesce. John Bright was ridiculed for defending the rights of the Barons of Oudh. Perhaps his political instinct was more true than the doctrinaire abstractions of those who sneered at him. At all events, I give no conclusions of my own, but those of the shrewdest and most experienced administrators, when I state these views. You have now in operation a vast bureaucratic system, based essentially upon Socialistic principles. Do not drive your abstract principles to the death. How badly you may fare by simply pressing supposed popular rights—which are often so only in name—may be seen in the action of the Municipal Councils. They are distrusted by all; are kept from more flagrant errors only by official guidance; and the fact that they are elected does not give them the confidence of the native in any degree whatever.

These are considerations which press upon any one who endeavours to catch the trend of official opinion—and, not less, of the best native opinion—as he passes from one station to another in India. But the outward aspect of things fixes our interest apart from all underlying political problems. From Agra I went on to Lucknow. It is there that we come within the real tragedy of the Mutiny. Of all Indian stations, it is one of the pleasantest and the most popular. With its handsome buildings, its well-ordered rows of shops, its large public parks, and the trim and well-timbered gardens of the military and civil lines, stretching along four or five miles of broad and well-kept roads, it is more European in appearance than any Indian town I have yet seen. But its cheery society, its pleasant life, its ample appurtenances of ornament and civic embellishment, are but a foreground to the tragedy that lies behind. The first public building I visited was the Martinière College, established after long lawsuits about 1845, under the will of General Claude Martin, the French soldier of fortune, who attained high position and wealth as an English officer, and dying in 1800, left this as one amongst the many public institutions which were to preserve his name. His school, erected as a Palace about 1786, in a most whimsical and almost grotesque fashion, which is a medley of barbaric pomp and the rococo of French eighteenth century taste, stands in a beautiful park, which is one of the many ornaments of Lucknow, and in its vaults the General's body rests. The edifice is strange enough for a school, but it serves its purpose fairly well, and it has gained from age and from its surroundings a certain beauty of its own. Its pupils are of European parentage born in India, and a certain number of Eurasians. There is always something of sadness in the lot of those who have never known their own country, and that sadness no educational contrivances can entirely remove. But the school is proud of its traditions, and creates a strong *esprit de corps* amongst its pupils; and it has acquired a special claim to respect and admiration for the memorable part which its pupils took in the defence of the Residency in 1857. Its loyalty is as strong to-day as it was fifty years ago.

I am not going to add one more to the countless descriptions of those landmarks of history which are the pride of Lucknow—the Alumbagh, with Havelock's grave; the Sekundrabagh, with its marks of the famous breach and its memories of righteous vengeance; the Kaisarabagh, with its emblems of the two Fishes, the arms of the House of Oudh, and its long rows of stately apartments, now used by the great native landholders during their visits to the town; above all, the wistful beauty and the sublime calm of the old Residency and its adjacent buildings—ruins beautiful in themselves, beautiful in their surroundings, and charged to the full with associations of heroism and of suffering which time can never efface. Nowhere have the tragic scenes of the Mutiny been toned into such loving harmony of colour and of feeling as in these thirty-five acres of lovely park, so quiet, so bathed in gentle lights, so softened to the spirit of mingled pride and sadness with which they affect any one with the smallest spark of imagination. As one is subdued to the spirit of the place, one wonders if, far off and amid all our distractions, we have fully grasped what our own fellow-countrymen and countrywomen suffered and dared during these long months of heroic struggle. If the lesson has faded from our memories, here at least it becomes irresistibly real, and sinks into our hearts with overwhelming force. Lucknow is now one of the favourite stations of India. It is bright and full of life, and welcomes us to its trim gardens, its well-ordered shops, the homelike cleanness and orderliness of its smiling gardens and bungalows. The vast native city, with its mean streets, its naked urchins, and its troops of privileged monkeys hopping from roof to roof, its dust and its disorder and its squalid poverty, is safely at a distance. But the background of the whole is one of pervading tragedy, and the memory of suffering and heroism is softened by time into a strange mixture of pride and sadness.

At Cawnpore we pass into a different scene. At Delhi every stone tells us of heroic fights and victory against overwhelming odds. At

Lucknow the element of sadness enters far more largely into the scene, but it is retrieved by the memory of final triumph. At Cawnpore there is nothing but unmitigated tragedy and the memory of the shambles. Cawnpore is not a place where one wishes to linger. In the town itself there is no attraction. It lies in the midst of what is now a barren tract of parched ground. Its streets present nothing on which the eye wishes to dwell. There are only two spots which one must visit, if it were only to pay the tribute due from every fellow-countryman to the memory of those who passed through the terrible martyrdom which yet fills the air with its horrors. We enter the gates of the garden where lies the memorial marking the site of the accursed well; and we feel the absolute fitness of the rule which prescribes that no carriage shall pass through that garden except at the pace of a hearse. Save for the gardeners weeding the grass lawns, no native is permitted within these gates, and the syce who sits behind our gharry alights and walks beside the carriage as it proceeds at a foot pace. We scarcely have a thought to spend on the artistic merits of the shrine that encircles the well; perfect simplicity is all we want; art can neither add to, nor detract from, the utter sadness of the scene and all its memories. The site of the house of Nana Sahib, where the deeds of horror were enacted, is wisely marked by nothing but a black marble slab; and close by lies the little graveyard enclosure, crowded with the hummocks of nameless graves, and by an occasional simple stone telling of husband, wife, and children done to death in this Aceldama. The shortest inscriptions are the best. No words can be more eloquent than the spot itself. We see the tree where some of the murderers were hanged, the spot where the guns stood from which others were blown to pieces; but all else is hushed except the memory of the tragedy. We realise at what a price India was held, and what are the horrors that wait upon errors of judgment or laxity of rule. It is a sight that may well silence rash comments and give pause to the frivolous criticism of those who hold that vast burden in their hands.

We pass beyond that garden of blood, and drive a mile or two farther, to where, beyond

General Wheeler's cantonment, the memorial church stands in the solemn quiet of a setting sun. A little farther on and we are passing down the road where the fated convoy had to pass to the ghaut, or landing-place, where they were to be betrayed and murdered. The Ganges is now a thin strip of water lying between wide-stretching sands, which, on that fatal day in June fifty years ago, were covered by its waters. The old landing-place, with its Hindu shrine, stands just as it did on that day. All round is silent, bare, and barren. The walls and banks, from which the defenceless crowd was shot down by those whose promises they trusted, stand in the gloomy scene like things accursed. There seems to be a blight over the whole dreary expanse, and it might be haunted by the ghosts of those that passed down those steps on that fatal morning. We are glad to be quit of Cawnpore and its memories; but it is vain to think that the lesson of these days can lightly be forgotten by those whose fellow-citizens have the same grim tragedy lying for ever within the possibilities of their life to-day.

XV

IN THE SACRED CITY

BENARES, *December* 30, 1907.

THERE are some curious features in the domestic economy of the official Anglo-Indian which one learns only by degrees. I have already spoken of the comparative equality of incomes and of the absence of any wealthy commercial class. But there are other conditions that tend still further to equalise the different grades of official rank. The native knows, with absolute accuracy, each step upward in his Sahib's career, and adjusts his own demands accordingly. As the official attains to the position of a *bara Sahib*, or great authority, the arrangements of his household change without any intervention by him. The duties which were performed by one servant now require two or more. The *chowkidar*, or watchman, who guarded the precincts of his house — a nondescript person, who is generally to be found peacefully reposing in the verandah, who really guards nothing, and who receives his pay as a sort of blackmail to the tribe of professional thieves to which he usually belongs—is multiplied by two or three. Each of the big Sahib's horses requires more fodder, and two syces are wanted where one sufficed before. The commission on all purchases—which is more deeply rooted than any religious tenet—represents a higher percentage. The Lat Sahib's (or Lord Sahib's) *khansama* commands the market, and in his own class is a personage of as much consideration as his master. But his weekly supplies augment automatically, and the price for each article swells in the same proportion. Remonstrance is absolutely useless. It is a fixed tradition which he is bound to maintain for the honour of his master, and with the most profound reverence and humility he professes himself powerless to alter it. Such things have always been so, and must so continue to the end of time; any alteration would shake the foundations of society.

If a drastic economist insisted upon a more business-like arrangement he would soon find himself circumvented by the wiles of omnipotent tradition; a lynx-eyed army of retainers would combine to teach him his social duties according to their own ideal.

This is only another of the many strange phases of official life in India. Its hospitality is boundless. There is a certain dignity in its surroundings which is unlike anything at home. Domestic details do not obtrude themselves as with us. Its machinery is carried on by a great silent host of retainers who adjust its *minutiæ* according to their own ideas, whose ways are hidden from us, and amongst whom there permeates the most minute personal knowledge both as to host and guest.

Of that official life, Allahabad, where I stayed after leaving Cawnpore, presents a fresh type. It is comparatively new, and the English quarter, or Canning-town, as it is called, was entirely built since the Mutiny days. In spite of the Mohammedan name imposed on it by Mogul conquerors it is still markedly Hindu both in population and in sympathy. Like most other towns in this part of India it was provided with a fort by Akbar, and although its architectural features have been much defaced, that fort still dominates the place, and stands on a splendid site at the confluence of the Ganges and the Jumna. These two rivers are now comparatively small and almost fordable on foot, but during the rainy season they must form a magnificent expanse of water. They irresistibly remind one of the junction of the Blue and White Nile at Khartoum. The confluence of the two rivers gives a sacred character to the spot, and each year it is the scene of a *mela*, or religious fair, which every twelfth year is of enormous dimensions. Last year it was calculated that no fewer than two millions of people gathered on the great plain that spreads beneath the fort. All sects—many of them bitterly antagonistic—gathered together in a dense crowd. Fakirs and priests worked themselves and their followers into a state of fanatical frenzy, and an eager mass of votaries pressed on in an insane fury to bathe in the sacred stream. Death in such circumstances would have been esteemed a blessed fate, and no thought of danger intervened to prevent fierce struggles between the contending crowds. Yet order was preserved by a small body of police, ably directed by the officials of the place, and only a small number of the vast horde which collected succumbed to this pressure of an apparently uncontrollable multitude; and so admirable were the sanitary arrangements that the whole of the camp was saved from what seemed an almost inevitable visitation of plague. At home we hear too little of such achievements, and know nothing of the foresight and labour that they involve.

Allahabad is not, then, so wanting in historical associations and in interesting relics as its adverse critics pretend. But it is its own peculiar character that gives to it its chief charm. Were we suddenly planted in it, without the intervening journeys, it would impress us chiefly by its calm and dignity, by the placid orderliness which we associate with an English cathedral city. Its long, wide roads, with their ample borders of foliage, have the quietude of an old-world scene. You pass along them for half a mile or more, without meeting more than a casual passenger or two. There is no rattle of traffic, no noise or crowding here. We are in the home of the High Court of the North-Western Provinces, as it is technically called; in reality, of the High Court of the United Provinces of Agra and Oudh. Here the legal element predominates over the administrative and the military; and it gives to the place a serene dignity that is all its own. Nowhere in India have we such a sense of restfulness; nowhere is there more of homelike comfort; and nowhere can we better realise that quiet sociability which we associate with the old pre-Mutiny days. Walk about the bandstand in the Park towards the evening, and in the quaint, old-fashioned carriages, in the mingled crowd of natives and of Anglo-Indians, you will find, not, perhaps, the lightsomeness and gaiety of a modern station, but the old-world friendliness and the quiet ease of a peaceable and well-ordered community.

I saw a good deal of the High Court itself, and was impressed by the succinct and admirably presented arguments of the pleaders, and the prompt discharge of business. In the Civil Court, the cases dealt with were all important appeals; and in some six or seven rather intricate cases judgment was pronounced at once, only a single case being reserved *ad avizandum*. But I was chiefly struck with one case of criminal appeal, which, to the Western mind, was sufficiently extraordinary, although I gather that it presented nothing very unusual to those versed in the strange ways of the native. A zemindar of rather a quarrelsome character had been found pilfering some crops in a neighbour's field. A dispute and struggle arose, and he was compelled to give up his plunder, the value of which was computed at two annas. The plundered person straightway went off to the police station, two miles away, to lodge a complaint. Meanwhile, the discomfited pilferer went to a field where his wife was working, with their six-years-old son. He attempted to strangle the boy, and was prevented only by the intervention of the neighbours. He then went home, and finding his infant daughter sleeping in a shed outside, he murdered her, and proceeded to hide the body in the compound of the neighbour with whom he had had the dispute; then raised a cry about her loss, and declared that he suspected his enemy of the murder, and himself aided in the search for the body and the chopper with which the murder had been committed, which, unfortunately for him, was proved to be his own. This method of vengeance, I was assured, is by no means uncommon; but the only doubt was whether the chain of evidence was not too complete, and whether it did not point to a concocted story, strung together by the native police and the witnesses against an obnoxious neighbour. The whole judgment of the Magistrate of first instance was directed to this point, and it showed by an admirable process of reasoning that the evidence linked itself together with a certainty too clear to be attained by any conspiracy. The sentence was confirmed, and doubt was really impossible. But it was a convincing proof of the impossibility of calculating the strange vagaries of the native mind upon any conception of what would appear probable or even possible to Western experience.

I must not, however, dwell longer upon the special charm of Allahabad, and the interest which it has as the centre of a great judicial system. From there I went to a very different scene in Benares, and one which is in just as striking contrast with anything that I had seen before. The contrast presents itself at once. Instead of a native town completely separated from the civil and military lines, you drive from the station through roads in which humble native shops and huts are intermingled with the villas of wealthy Hindus and the bungalows of the Anglo-Indians. Every now and then you come on a spacious mansion surrounded by ample gardens, where some notable Hindu Maharajah has his occasional abode in the sacred city. The Maharajah of Benares has no independent power, but he is treated with high consideration, is entitled to the honour of a salute of guns, and holds that respect with which the native regards the representative of an ancient family. We have here, in short, a city where the tradition of hereditary rank, the concourse of the devout, and the sanctity of a spot where the Hindu worship is a dominating influence, all combine to counterbalance the supremacy of the official authority. Only a little more than a hundred miles apart, no two cities are more unlike than Allahabad and Benares.

It was in the lengthening shadows of the late afternoon that we drove out to the shrine at Sarnath, some three miles out from the city, where the Buddhist traditions are still supreme, and where, in the third century B.C., the Buddhist Emperor Asoka built a great monastery and adorned it with all that was finest in Hindu art. It opens up a new treasure-house of Indian antiquities. One thing strikes us most of all—how far we are from the creations of Mogul art that have filled our eye so long. At Lahore, at Delhi, at Agra, at Allahabad, we have seen the stately proportions, the delicate tracery, the unrivalled beauty of conventional design. Here we are in touch with all the harmonious grace of Greek art, rich with statues of the human figure and lifelike presentations of the animal world. Mohammedan restrictions here count for nothing, and in the large collection of sculptured figures, stored in a shed close by, we are constantly lighting on the emblems of Hindu worship, treated with all the grace and living vigour of Hellenic art. After a long diet of Mogul remains this glimpse of truer and more living creation comes as a sensible relief.

But, after all, this is not the most characteristic aspect of Benares. In the supremely sacred city of India the real interest is one of to-day; and it is to be found in that part of the city which stretches along the broad waters of the Ganges. In the early morning we drive through miles of streets where humble dwellings and shabby booths are mingled with considerable mansions, and take boat at a ghaut at the extreme west of the city. There, in the brilliant light of the rising sun, and with a background of multi-coloured mist, we have spread before us a scene which more than realises the most imaginative creations of Turner. Tier after tier of lofty staircase, surmounted by massive masonry, and ending in gilded minarets, tower above the glittering waters of the Ganges. Along the river there are countless brown figures of the bathers, and up and down the steps there is moving a constant crowd of figures clad in all the colours of the rainbow, the orange-coloured shawls of the priests predominating. Along the edge of the stream are passing a succession of boats of a pattern thousands of years old. Here and there the mighty stairs have crumbled to the water's edge, and a confused mass of temples and carved pinnacles remain standing at every angle, still beautiful in their quaint carving, and adorned with fantastic devices. The waters now lap their bases, but in the rainy season often rush in a swirling current some thirty or forty feet higher up their massive masonry, and sap its foundations. Ever and again we come to spots where the pyres for the dead are smouldering, and where the corpses, clad in strange clothing, lie ready for the torch. It is a sight we might dream of, but which we would never think to see in sober reality. Here we are at the very centre of the heart of India. Come nearer to the crowd, and amongst the bathers you will discern the faces of the humble labourer, of the ascetic fakir, of the shrewd pundit, and of the wealthy merchant, all mingled in the throng. In this mystic scene, which seems to rise before us in the changing sunlight like a vision from dreamland, and yet throbbing with all the keenness of a strenuous and enthusiastic energy, we see a type of all that fervent and yet remote Oriental life, against which the waves of Western thought beat in vain, and amidst which the chatter of the political theories of to-day sounds strangely inept and ineffectual.

XVI

OUR EDUCATIONAL WORK AND ITS RESULTS

CALCUTTA, *January* 2, 1908.

THE sight of Benares, and its local conditions, suggest some curious thoughts as to the aim and purpose of our Indian Administration in one particular. Many of the problems it presents are far too difficult for definite pronouncement; but above all it prompts us to think of the means which we employ to impress upon the vast mass the imprint of Western civilisation, and how far this is a task within human power. We have entered with some confidence upon schemes of Western education, and one is tempted to ask what are the prospects of success, and what has been the actual result. At Benares the problem presents itself with something of special significance. Perhaps I may be pardoned for finding in it one also of special interest.

A wise observer, of long experience, said to me the other day, "It would have been a happy thing for India had Macaulay never lived." Such a heresy will make the orthodox Whig aghast with horror. I would not venture to propound it, but I cannot help recognising that it has some justification. It is with Macaulay's name that the foundations of our educational system in India are associated. It took its rise at a time when educational ideals found their hopes of realisation in examination and the competitive system, and when no inconvenient doubts existed as to the infallibility of Western methods. We have learned much since then; and above all we have learned to distrust some of the most cherished axioms, and to see that we must follow nature, and not fetter her: that we must adapt ourselves to the material with which we have to deal. We have found that education means something more than imparting information or developing a few intellectual aptitudes, and that, if it is to be effective, its chief work must be to build up character.

But the great work of education in India was taken in hand just when doubts were ignored; when the crude theories which gave us London University of the early Victorian days were in full vogue; and when a South Kensington, with its annual crop of so-called qualified teachers as its crowning result, was looked upon as the main hope of national development. That time has not long passed away, but we have safely left it behind us at home. It dominated our scheme for India, and there its bondage is still strong.

What did we set ourselves to do? We felt no doubt as to the ultimate dominance of Western ideas and of Western thought. Some of the older Western ideals were abandoned, and a brand-new system, which seemed to be the very acme of perfection, was planted upon India. Modern philosophy was to be carted over in all its freshest developments, and Macaulay, for one, felt confident that before its brilliant light all Eastern thought would grow pale and vanish out of existence. What was called political science was to be imparted to a race whose centuries of history made them regard all its maxims as elaborate and unsubstantial fancies. The ingenuity and the imitativeness of the Oriental mind made it easy for these maxims to be turned to deft uses, while, as a real or practical system, it played only on the surface of their minds. The teaching of English literature was a favourite subject with the educational reformers of the day; so it was dumped upon India with complacent self-confidence. Above all, the English language was conceived to be the great instrument of civilisation; so it was made a universal and compulsory subject in all schemes of higher education. It was forgotten that the strain and struggle of Western life was imparting to us at home a practical education independent of all our schools and Colleges, and that for India the first business of education was to develop that practical side which lay buried beneath a vast load of Oriental tradition and prejudice. Our grandfathers thought that all religious difficulties could be safely solved by the principles of Whig latitudinarianism. So ancient faiths were tolerated in India, but with the toleration of indifference. A common standard was to be maintained by a vast system of examinations and prescribed curricula, whose yoke is a heavy burden in India to this day, and which develop all that is worst in the Oriental mind.

On most Indian questions I form an opinion with diffidence and express it with hesitation. On the main aspects of the educational question I confess that I feel less hesitation. I have seen much earnest and energetic work, and I am conscious that there is much more that I have not seen. But in thinking that in its main lines it is hopelessly wrong I am only repeating the opinion expressed to me universally by all the wisest Anglo-Indians and natives whom I have seen, and impressed on me by my own experience. I can only describe that impression by saying that there is a sort of mildew lying over the work. System, routine, and formality rest like shackles over the whole thing. I found handbooks of the modern philosophy of the West in the hands of whole class-rooms of students, who could formally con their teachings, but in whose minds a totally different set of thoughts were implanted by their history and their nature. Theories of political science and of political economy were being inculcated in youths who could deftly apply them to their own purposes, but who were entirely ignorant that the matters which they discussed and the theories which they propounded were not fundamental axioms, but matters on which in Western life a hundred different views were entertained. One of the ablest amongst the educational workers whom I have met told me, with the weariness of misapplied labour, "I have to-day been trying to explain to a class of Hindu students the meaning of Shelley's *Ode to the Skylark* and *Silas Marner*. They are prescribed in the University curriculum, and so they must be learned. What good can it do?" Only one answer is possible. In the libraries of the higher schools I constantly found *Tom Brown's School Days*. What meaning can that have for boys who have drunk in with their mother's milk ideas of formal courtesy, of studied respect for age and rank, of a personal dignity dependent on fixed rules which have the force of religion? Do we really imagine that we shall create in them the spirit of the English schoolboy by what they must hold to be a travesty of all the relations of life as these appear to them?

I am quite aware that there is a good deal of sound technical education being attempted in India, and I am glad to know that some of the ablest of our Indian administrators feel the necessity of more being done in this way. But in many cases I am obliged to confess that such technical education as I saw was a miserable mockery, and those who showed it could only say that they had hopeless hindrances—the weight of which I fully admit—to contend against. The system of caste, the habits of the people, their inertness in manual labour, their fixed idea that clerical work has a dignity of its own—all these will take long before they are overcome. But meanwhile we might surely endeavour to link the intellectual training which we give more closely to their life and their traditions, and to abandon the senseless attempt to turn an Oriental into a bad imitation of a Western mind. Why should we teach them that education is impossible without acquiring the

English language? What can that impress upon them, except that education is useful only to enable them to undertake those administrative duties which are their absorbing ambition, and in the exercise of which they rarely command the confidence of their own race? Here in Bengal, under the Permanent Settlement of Lord Cornwallis, the great zemindars have large estates and vast influence. The management of these estates and the supervision of their tenants or ryots might give them employment of the best kind and a sphere of enormous usefulness. If education is to do anything for them, it must be by making them cultivated gentlemen, of enlarged views, but not necessarily views out of harmony with their own traditions. As it is, they leave our Colleges with only one aim, to become Government officials, and with acquisitions of knowledge that drive them further from their own people, instead of bringing them into closer touch with, and rendering them more fit for, the work which can be discharged by none except themselves. It is not a triumph for our education—it is, on the contrary, a satire upon it—when we find the sons of leading natives expressly discouraged by their parents from acquiring any knowledge of the vernacular. Yet instances of this are by no means rare. It is a smaller thing, but yet an undoubted evil, that this overstrained temptation to the native to learn English tends to render the command of the vernacular by Anglo-Indians much more restricted than the old officials assure us that it was in the early days of their service. This does not, of course, apply to the provincial districts—the *Mofussil*, as they are called, where the district officer must be, and is, familiar with the vernacular—but it is unquestionably the case in some of the central seats of government. If the tendency spreads, it will sap more than anything else the security of our hold on India. It is one of the chief incentives to a certain class of natives to acquire facility in our tongue, that by so doing they can interpose between the higher official class and the mass of the people.

I am quite aware of the immense difficulties of recasting the educational system. But that it requires recasting is the opinion, not of a man here and there, but of every one who is capable of judging. We must free education from the domination of examinations. We must leave greater freedom of choice and of method to separate Colleges and schools. We must show the native that education has other aims than to make Babus, subordinate officials, and pleaders. We must teach them that there are other spheres of activity for the educated man than the Law Courts and Government appointments. We must abandon the vain dream that we can reproduce the English public school on Indian soil. We must recognise that it is a mistake to insist that a man shall not be considered to be an educated man unless he can express his knowledge in a language which is not his own. Place no restriction on English as an optional subject, but cease to demand it as the one thing necessary for all.

And in another and a more restricted sphere, I fancy that most of those who know India will agree that, with the most benevolent of aims, we have encouraged a course of doubtful expediency. It has become the fashion for the sons of well-to-do parents to be sent to Britain for their education, and educational institutions at home are not slow to encourage it. But is it wise, and does it tell in the long run, for their own good or the good of their country? Such youths come into surroundings for which, as a rule, they are ill-fitted. With the marvellous capacity which they possess of adapting themselves to the superficial aspects of their surroundings, they settle down for a time, and their tutors and guides at home are satisfied with their conduct, and fancy that they are being moulded into British shape. But do they enter with full sympathy into our thoughts and feelings, or is it, indeed, expedient that they should do so, in view of their future lives? They usually come when, with a maturity strange to the Western youth, they are at the same time utterly incapable of judging our social conditions, or knowing them below the surface. Too often they form aspirations which can never be satisfied, and which no human contrivance can enable them to attain without involving incalculable evil. They break with their own traditions; they cease to be true representatives of their own people, and yet they are divided by an impassable barrier from ours. I know that there are notable exceptions, but they are due to special natural faculties and to special racial peculiarities. For the most part the experiment of mental and moral acclimatisation proves a hopeless failure. Let them come, if they come at all, not at the impressionable period of youth, but when character has been formed, and when they are able to judge and to appreciate, not to imitate superficial traits.

I wish most carefully to guard myself against any suspicion of adversely criticising the educational officials of India. Some of them, I fancied, seemed tired out with their work, and scarcely to be versed in the most recent educational movements. But amongst them there are men of first-rate ability. It is the system that is wrong—wrong in its original conception, and faulty in its present administration. Education has no independent place in the central Secretariat, and all new schemes must be submitted through an alien department. The result is what it inevitably must be—misunderstanding and delay. The evil was supposed to be met some years ago by the appointment of a junior official from home, to act as a sort of general adviser to the Central Government. The plan was one which, without the smallest personal reflection, hardly could have proved satisfactory, and which has not apparently worked better than was to be expected. I had the advantage of hearing some of the educational evidence placed before the Decentralisation Commission which is now ranging over India. The chief witness examined (of whom I knew nothing before) seemed to me to give his evidence with admirable force, and was evidently in touch with all that is soundest in educational theory at home. It is not, perhaps, surprising that his questioners were not so conspicuously conversant with the subject; and the cross-examination of one of the Commissioners—himself a civil servant in India—served what was to me the useful purpose of showing a spirit which, so long as it prevails in official quarters, will, in my opinion, effectually bar the way against any real educational reform. Educational administration must have its own independent position before it can make any bold and effective advance.

XVII

CALCUTTA

CALCUTTA, *January* 2, 1908.

IT is a strange experience to reach Calcutta after spending a couple of months in travelling over the country, and seeing India on the *Mofussil* or provincial side, and in the "jungly" districts. As you go south-eastwards through Bengal, the country changes rapidly. In place of the boundless parched plains and the stinted herbage, you pass through thickets of palms, through leafy tropical vegetation, and past tanks and channels of water that are lying under a heavy vapour in the early dawn. At length, after the usual tedious and heart-breaking delays, the train, crowded with those who have been able to escape for a few days from the weary bondage of incessant work to the

Christmas festivities of Calcutta, creeps into Howdrah Station, which might almost be mistaken for a London terminus. Last night we were amongst the strange scenes of Benares, repeating in all their main features what must have been the life of thousands of years; this morning we are passing through crowded and bustling streets which, but for the dominance of dark faces, might belong to any European capital. Electric tramways run in all directions; motor omnibuses meet us here and there; the commercial European is in evidence on every side; English policemen are to be seen at each street corner; and in the principal thoroughfares there are the bustle and strain of a busy day in the City.

In some respects Calcutta is in sharp contrast with Bombay. At Bombay one is chiefly struck by the variety of the motley throng, by the picturesque and brilliant colouring, by the entirely Oriental aspect of the place, and by the rare occurrence of a white face amidst all the passing crowd. Here in Calcutta it is quite different. The English tongue is constantly in your ear. The commerce is, to all intents and purposes, entirely in English hands. The Bengali does not trust the honesty or the capacity of his fellow-Bengali, and will not invest his money in enterprises which Bengali management controls. Instead of variety, there is a great monotony in the native type, and, in outward appearance at least, that type is not prepossessing. It is in marked contrast with the physical strength and manliness of the up-country races. Except when they gather for a festivity—to watch a race or a polo competition, both of which attract them marvellously—the natives here do not affect bright-coloured garments. The crowds that gather in the Maidan for any festivity are certainly brilliant enough in colour, and look at a distance like a vast parterre of richly varied flower-beds. But the effect of bright colour is chiefly due to those who throng to these gatherings belonging to other parts of India, and who, in the streets and in their common occupations, use a more sombre garb. The Bengali, with his regular features, his poorly developed physique, his aspect of a town loiterer, his carefully trimmed and heavily oiled hair, his most ineffective and untidy of all garments—the dhootie—which waggles about his legs and leaves the backs of them bare, and yet not free for active exercise; above all, with his effeminate sunshade—is in wondrous contrast with the Sikh of the Punjab—even more still with the Pathan of the Northern Frontier, to whose aspect one's eyes have become accustomed. It is only in the Viceroy's splendid bodyguard that you see that type repeated in Calcutta.

A Calcutta crowd does not show the same brightness of colour and the same teeming variety as Bombay. Nor can Calcutta boast the splendid sea front which gives to Bombay its claim to rank amongst the fairest cities of the world. But besides its busy, energetic, vigorous life, and its aspect of solid prosperity, Calcutta has one invaluable possession—the finest expanse of open ground in its great Maidan of which any city can boast. How many cities possess a park stretching from the very heart of the business quarter for miles beyond, and ending in a splendid racecourse, yet all encompassed by populous districts of the town, which spread round it in all directions, and which can all equally partake in this magnificent pleasure ground? The Maidan is the very salvation of Calcutta. Never has posterity had greater reason to bless the foresight of those who planned the lines of an extending Calcutta, and who provided her with a lung without which she would be a centre of malaria, and hopeless as a dwelling-place. As it is, she draws her very life from the Maidan, and from the fair gardens and recreation grounds that spread out round her in the beautiful country beyond, and along the reaches of the upper river.

But although it cannot rival the beauty of the sea view of Bombay, and does not equal it in brilliancy of colour, Calcutta has a massiveness and an impression of energy which are all its own. The river gives no glimpses of picturesque buildings. Stacks of factory chimneys hide the finer aspects of the city as you pass along the Hoogly between masses of shipping which would recall the Thames below London Bridge were it not for the ungainly hulks of the "flats," as they call the flat-bottomed, shapeless Brobdingnagian floating vans which carry on the coasting trade with Eastern Bengal. It is only when we have passed through miles of factories and grimy trading vessels that we shake off the city and come back to rural India—to stately temples, to wide leafy stretches, and to the spacious villas where the Calcutta merchant princes of an older day had their abode. The remnants of some of these may be seen close to the city, where an occasional piece of decorated architecture or of neglected garden may be detected amidst the masses of factories, before whose advance they have been trampled down. One of these mouldering Palaces was occupied by the King of Oudh when his long misdoings ended in his deposition, and he was brought down to be kept in safe custody at Calcutta. To-day the river view of Calcutta gives us the impression of a vast manufacturing city. Only forty or fifty years ago it was merely a great shipping port, and none of these stacks of chimneys were to be seen. In place of them there must have been long lines of the spacious villa residences of the merchants of Calcutta, who found on the river bank a favourite place of residence, from which they have gradually been displaced. Such villas are now to be found far across the Maidan in the English quarter. Nothing could be more unlike the usual English lines of a provincial station in India than the houses which we meet with there. We might fancy ourselves in one of the best types of London suburb—as the better London suburb was some forty years ago. Hampton Court, Richmond, or Twickenham, of the sixties, had many scenes exactly like the English quarter of Calcutta to-day. It is a long series of comfortable villas, sometimes of stately mansions, each with some garden ground around it, and with the restfulness and dignity of abundant space. But the jerry-builder has planted his foot in Calcutta, and is working his dire purposes with it. Great tenements of flats are rising, and complaints are rife of rising rents and scarcity of houses. The next step will be rows of crescents and of terraces, and then the Calcutta of our fathers will be a thing of the past. Life in Calcutta now is gay and energetic, and takes a reflection of brightness and joyousness from the very sunlight in which it is perpetually bathed. But it must have been more stately and reposeful in the olden days, when the factories were not, when the air was smokeless, when the great business houses were few and less flaunting in their architecture. They often comprised the mansion of the commercial magnate, who dwelt beside his work, and it is from one such home surviving, a dignified centre of hospitality, amidst younger and less attractive surroundings, in the very centre of the business quarter, that I have had my first glimpse of Calcutta under the happiest auspices. In those olden days the official and mercantile classes were more fused together than is now the case. Here we are at the centre of official India, where the hand of the greater administrators is on the pulse of every provincial government, and is shaping the policy of the whole. The outward semblance of officialism is nowhere so imposing, nor is its real authority anywhere so great. Yet here one feels something of the atmosphere of home in the relations of the official and the non-official element. Elsewhere the official is everything, the rest is nothing. Here the official is great, but beyond his sphere of influence there lies—almost as in England—a vast population that gives scarcely a thought to the doings of the official world from year's end to year's end. To the native of the *Mofussil* the "Commissioner Sahib" is a visible Providence; to the Calcutta merchant he is as little known as a Commissioner of Inland Revenue is to the ordinary London citizen.

During the Christmas week Calcutta is not only the gathering-place of all India: it is the meeting-place of travellers from every quarter of the globe. The festivities have nothing of the homely and intimate familiarity, and the tolerance of makeshift resources, which one sometimes sees in the *Mofussil*, and which really gives its tenderest and most moving significance to the scanty breaks in the strenuous life of these parts. The balls and entertainments of the Calcutta Christmas week rival those of London. The races might compare with the most important fixtures in England, and we have had polo competitions which leave all that we might see elsewhere hopelessly outstript. In the gay crowd we no doubt come across many of the strained and preoccupied faces that reflect the realities and the anxieties of Indian official life. But they are mixed—nay, they are overwhelmed —with crowds of gaily dressed visitors, with the Jewish financier from Paris, with the German merchant, with the tourist who sees in India nothing but a place where some new distraction may be found for a few weeks, and with the usual nondescript denizens of every racecourse. This at least may be safely said, that nowhere in the world will they find they can take their pastime so pleasantly as on the racecourse in the great Maidan of Calcutta.

The life of Calcutta is that of a great commercial community, living on perfectly easy terms, but in no close intimacy, with a strong but comparatively small official circle. Beyond them both there lies the great surrounding mass of natives, ministering to them, living on them, leading a separate life, and with very little of the cheeriness and easy courtesy that one meets with farther afield. The native in the streets of Calcutta strikes me as sulky in demeanour, disagreeable as a passenger, and having neither the instinctive courtesy of the Oriental nor the good-humoured give-and-take which one meets with, as a rule, in the streets at home. He would be a dangerous element in an unruly crowd.

Calcutta, on the whole—except for its sun—is marvellously like home. One constantly meets those whose home it is, and who know nothing else of India. Nothing is more certain than that, to such as these, India is practically unknown. They are here at the centre of the vast and complex machine of administration. But for the real understanding of the problems with which that administration has to deal, Calcutta by itself would teach us less than nothing. But if we think of all the vast issues that are here controlled, it is a focus of surpassing interest.

XVIII

CALCUTTA IN RETROSPECT

S.S. "SUMATRA," CALCUTTA TO CEYLON,
January 8, 1908.

IT is a strange contrast from the bustle and vigorous life of Calcutta to find oneself dropping quietly down the Hoogly between banks overgrown with a mass of tropical jungle. Our progress is leisurely, not to say sleepy; the channel is difficult; the shifting tide requires us to come to an anchor more than once, and at times one can scarcely perceive that the boat is moving, except by watching the banks gradually receding, until only a vast expanse of water stretches on every side, and we see land as two threadlike lines on the starboard and the port. The blazing sun and the breathless air help the feeling of slumbrous quiet. We seem to have passed into a different world; and the crowded streets, the rattling tikka-gharries, the noise of the coolies at the wharf, seem to have been left ages behind us. Still further in the background lies the memory of the long tracts of arid land between Bombay and the Punjab, far away north to the Khyber, and back to the sea at Calcutta. More than four thousand miles of that land have passed before our eyes, and each mile of them had something new to show, in spite of all their seeming monotony.

In the wide stretches of the Hoogly, with its slimy waters and the dreary monotony of its receding banks, India shows at its very worst. The channel permits only of progress at a snail's pace, while all navigation must be stopped at night. Over its waters there hangs a pestilent haze, now of sweltering heat, and now of penetrating cold. The energy seems to be taken out of every living thing except the mosquitoes, which show a fiendish activity. One would do much to avoid a railway journey across India, but the Hoogly exacts from you a heavy tax for this release.

I have attempted in these notes to give

little more than the impressions *de voyage*, as they fell upon untutored eyes, and I have written with a full consciousness of the absurdity of over-confident opinions upon questions which call for the experience of a lifetime of familiarity. But no British subject can divest himself of a certain responsibility for the vast problems of the Indian Empire; and rightly or wrongly, wisely or unwisely, the ultimate judgment thereon must rest at Westminster. Few, I think, can doubt that the affairs of India will, in the future, occupy not less, but more, of the attention of Parliament. If we cannot cure our ignorance, and even though we must be cautious in judgment, we may at least, after mingling in converse for months with those who know most, and can judge best, form some idea of what the main questions at issue are, and estimate, to some extent, the leading varieties of opinion that are held. We can, at least, begin to apprehend where the seed-plots of danger lie, and what mischief rash utterances may cause. That we can do little more does not absolve us from the duty of doing that.

At Calcutta there is doubtless concentrated

much of the best official opinion in India, and it is necessarily in close touch with the various provinces which are ably represented there. But the authorities there would probably be the last to claim that their views should be taken as an epitome of the whole. On the other hand, public opinion at Calcutta outside the official ranks would be in some ways the most unsafe of all guides to follow. Amongst the commercial class there are a few who know the country intimately, and judge its conditions with prudence, insight, and long practical knowledge. But the general society is largely composed of men who know Calcutta alone, and, as a consequence—to quote the words used to me by a Calcutta man—"know less about India than most educated men in London." The ordinary business man is not in touch with the native. In many instances he knows scarcely a word of his language. Yet on the broad questions of social relations and of political agitation he often speaks with far more of confidence, while carrying far less of conviction, than any official who has spent half a dozen years in an up-country district.

Some of the leading commercial men gave me views of very great value; but their value was in proportion to their diffidence and their caution. Too often one hears in those circles which are scarcely nearer to the heart of India than London is, a recklessness of talk which makes the wisest administrator shudder. They will confidently teach the officer of the native army the real truth as to disaffection amongst his men; and they will settle with easy dogmatism questions which puzzle the oldest official. You hear, with irritating frequency, words about "the ruling race" which never pass the lips of the responsible official. One difference between Calcutta and the *Mofussil* strikes one at once. So far as immediate personal danger is concerned, or any dread of things even worse than personal danger, they are no more present in Calcutta than in London. There may be plots and riots there. We have them at home. But unrest in the provinces is a real and ever-present menace—and by so much the less is it apt to be talked of. You *feel* that it is there, rather than hear of it. Those at home do not hear of it, and for that reason do not sufficiently realise the feeling. But it is there all the same, not as a source of nervousness or timidity, but as a summons to unremitting watchfulness. Yet here in Calcutta, and in Bengal generally, there is, beyond a doubt, the central machinery of political agitation. In other parts it takes various forms, and its intensity is felt in very different degrees. On the North-West Frontier it is working near the powder magazine of Pathan lawlessness and proneness to Mussulman fanaticism. Amongst the ranks of our native army it might easily find suitable soil, if we were ever to forget, or if we did not, indeed, carefully encourage, that feeling of *izat*, or instinctive self-respect and high-spirited pride, which is the chief guard of their loyalty. In the Punjab it stirs the poorer agriculturist by defaming official efforts, by fostering discontent against the Lands Alienation Act, and by decrying the administration of the canal colonies. In the United Provinces it can appeal to a class prone in any case to lawlessness and crime, and it may excite some sympathy amongst the talukdars or big landlords, who think their rights are being filched away from them in favour of the poor tenant. In Bengal it appeals to religious antipathy against the Mohammedans, to fancied interference with landlord rights, and to a class hard pressed by economic changes; and it can call to its aid a restless, turbulent, pampered host of Bengali lads, who are stirred to violence—so one is apt to suspect—by those whose public acts do not bring them within the law. Nothing is more certain than that the wires of all the agitation throughout the *Mofussil*, far and near, are pulled in Bengal.

There is nothing impresses one more in any attempt to study Indian conditions than the wide contrasts between the economics of the different provinces as regards the land. The most ordinary nomenclature tells you this. In the Punjab, the zemindar class in ordinary talk means the agricultural class generally, of which the vast majority are actual tillers of the soil. In Bengal, the zemindar is a landlord, and often a man who has waxed rich by the rack-renting of the ryot, under the conditions of Lord Cornwallis's Permanent

Settlement. The meaning of the word is simply "landholder"; but in the Punjab the tiller of the soil is, as a rule, the landholder; in Bengal he is the ryot.

Add to this central difference innumerable others — different proportions of race and religion, different character and physique, different customs and traditions—which divide one province from another, and you begin to understand not only the skill with which agitation is engineered, but its essential artificiality.

Who, then, are the chief engineers, and what is the foundation upon which they work? No native advocate of the schemes of the moderate, or even of the extreme party, will admit that he hopes or seeks for the ending of British rule. The moderates and extremists are not terms of very definite meaning, and on the fringes of both parties there are many who rank themselves according to an easy opportunism. Talking to an Englishman, every man will profess to be a moderate. In his public utterances every man will use words which can readily be interpreted by the extremist as favouring his views. It is doubtful how far the breach which occurred between the two during the Congress at Surat was for the advantage of settled rule or not. That there are, and that there are understood to be, two wings of the party, is far from an inconvenience to those who wish to extend its influence. But that there is a vast mass of ignorant native feeling, which vaguely looks for complete release from the white man's rule, and which would be stirred by no other appeal, in which the memory of old days is working, and who think that destiny is somehow on their side—this is absolutely certain. Equally certain it is that there are passages in many of the speeches which one reads every day which have no meaning, except as appeals to this vague longing and underlying ambition, and that secret missives are being distributed widely in the vernacular, which are addressed avowedly and expressly to that feeling. I have seen some such papers which chance has occasionally brought to light, and no one can estimate how far or how deeply their influence is working.

Very probably the educated or pleader

class, from which the incendiaries are chiefly drawn, do not themselves indulge in such aspirations, although they are compelled to encourage them implicitly. They have to find more specious matter of appeal, and to present it in a form in which it will attract the support of those who indulge in wilder expectations. I have already spoken of the religious movement, known as the Arya Somaj. It may be doubted whether, amongst the educated Hindus, any religious movement would now have much influence; and the childish religious superstitions of the ignorant mass would not probably be attracted by what claims to be a liberalising and rationalising of the old beliefs. But any religious propaganda will rouse a certain interest, and it at least draws a convenient line of demarcation between the white man and the native, and between the Hindu and the Mohammedan. We have only to recall the vast consequences of the religious movement that paved the way for the Sikh conquests, to realise how potent such a movement may become on this soil.

The next topic is Swadeshi, or the exclusive use of native products and native manufacture. This is a movement with which, within proper limits, and apart from any concomitant violence or boycott, every one to whom I have spoken professes sympathy. It is not illegitimate as an aspiration, nor even as a practical line of conduct, and it might not be economically inexpedient. But there is no doubt whatever that it has been enforced by means which flagrantly defied the law, and that these means have brought about collisions between Hindu crowds and Mohammedan traders, which are expressly contrived to make the interference of authority necessary, and to saddle that authority with the suspicion of discouraging native industry. If a popularly elected legislature were to enforce the principle compulsorily, it could only do so at the cost of an internecine war.

A further irritating topic, which may be openly discussed without direct sedition, is the Partition of Bengal. The grounds for this have long ago been stated, fully and convincingly. It was based upon unanswerable administrative reasons, and it was a necessity in order that just attention should be paid to the needs of Eastern Bengal. Of course, such a change interfered with some existing interests, and all these might be counted to swell the opposition. One educated and fair-minded native citizen of Calcutta professed his opposition to the partition. But he frankly admitted that the administrative reasons for it were sound, and that his own opposition was based on the fear that it would make Chittagong a dangerous rival port to Calcutta. I have read long and edifying appeals to sentiment, which are hollow platitudes, and carry their own refutation. It is asserted that the ryot is bitter in his opposition. That is about as likely as that the farm labourer of Kent or Sussex would be roused to indignation over the dissolution of the partnership between the South-Eastern and the London and Chatham Railways. Even natives who profess to belong to the "reform" party quietly smiled when the suggestion was made. On the other hand, I was assured by a prominent native member of Council, who is a distinguished leader of the moderates, that this was the one matter which lay at the root of all the discontent, and he urged its abandonment with an energy of enthusiasm which seemed to me to be rather overdone. His arguments were not such as carried conviction, and his whole position showed some lack of humour. It briefly amounted to this, "Let Government surrender to us in regard to a point which they claim to have decided on grounds of administrative efficiency, and we shall for ever be their most warm supporters and faithful subjects, and all difficulties will disappear." No doubt; and with his thanks we would equally gain the respect of the Mohammedans, to whom the partition means some equalising of opportunities, and the gratitude of the Punjabi zemindar, who must be so vitally interested in the question!

Is it altogether uncharitable to suppose that an agitation thus supported, and making more or less vague appeals to such diverse sympathies—between which it is hard to discern one point of contact—has for its main object the advancement of the interests of its leading agents? That the pleader class—the product of an artificial and ill-conceived system of education—and those who are most closely in sympathy with it, are the chief promoters of unrest is as certain as evidence can make it. No doubt they can safely say, as some of them have assured me, that the end of British authority is the last thing that they wish. It does not follow that they may not be appealing to instinctive longings that go further. Still less does it follow that they understand British rule as we do. If it is to be maintained, they would have it exploited for their own behoof. By its help they are to assume a position which their fellow-countrymen would not for a moment accord to them. They would have representative institutions, which their deft management and glib oratory would capture for themselves. By means of such machinery, and with the support of British authority, they would manipulate India, and impose on it an administrative tyranny worse than any from which it has suffered in past centuries. Of all the curses that pursue India, the worst is that of the subordinate native official, and it is that which the native chiefly abhors. The greatest blessing that could come to the country would be the deporting of the whole wretched tribe, down to the humblest red-coated chaprassi, who waits at the Sahib's door, extorts bribes for every admission to "the Presence," grinds his countrymen under his ignoble bullying, and ascribes it all—no doubt with perfect success—to the orders of the Sahib. He it is who poisons the wells of our administration, and presents it in the ugliest colours to the credulous native. And all the time he is growing rich on it, and shows it in that increased oiliness and obesity which always mark the prosperous native. It is easy to exhort the stamping out of this plague spot. I wish those who do so could listen to the countless stories of patient, but hopeless, effort on the part of officials who have tried. Drastic action, prompt punishment, vigilant protection of the sufferer, endless devices to outwit the petty bully—all end at last one way. The sufferer sooner or later comes to petition the Presence to relax his efforts, to allow him to pay the exaction, and to leave him the submissive victim of his bully before the breach of the sacred tradition of bribery has slowly worked his ruin.

I give only one story out of many. A Deputy Commissioner, convinced that a heavy commission was extorted by his own subordinates on account of all his appointments, contrived a means of outwitting them. At the next nomination of a village *lumbadar*, after deciding on his man, he called to the Babu on the spot for the formal certificate of appointment, which usually was made out and delivered the next day—of course, for a consideration. The paper was not forthcoming, although his orders had been clear, and this was, of course, owing to the fault of the subordinate's subordinate, who was duly rated by his immediate superior, with the usual lurid reflections upon the moral character of his progenitors, male and female. At last, after exasperating delay, the paper was made out, and presented to the newly appointed *lumbadar*, who received it with a mixture of wonder and embarrassment. He protested, pleaded custom, would be more than satisfied to receive it to-morrow, and would only take it when peremptorily ordered to do so and to go straight home. The subordinates were reprimanded and fined, and received both fine and reprimand as proving the eminent justice of the Presence, and as more than deserved on their part. No such delay would ever again merit the Sahib's just indignation.

Next year the Deputy returned to the district. On his arrival no preparations were made. There was no provender for his camels; the wood was damp, and would not burn; milk was not procurable; and no notice of his coming had been given. All was due to the wicked *lumbadar*, who was reported to have met all expostulation by scornful defiance of the Presence and of all the Sahibs. The *lumbadar* was summoned, and meekly acknowledged all his faults, and all the impious reflections which he had made on the Presence. He would make amends, and the like would never occur again. The Sahib's excellent Babus would, he hoped, forgive him.

The whole of the little plot was only too transparent. But expostulation, exhortation, assurance of protection—all were in vain. The only prayer of the poor *lumbadar*, in the end, was that the Presence, who was his father and his mother, would suffer him to come to terms with the Babus. If not, worse would befall him next year. Heavier charges would be brought against him, and would be supported by irrefragable evidence, which even the Presence could not disregard; and his ruin would be complete.

There is not a Deputy Commissioner in India who could not tell you just such a tale. Is the extension of this kind of thing the object of national aspiration, which we are to satisfy at the certain cost of civil war, the renewal of the old days of blood and anarchy, and the ruin of our work in India? But these subordinate officials, it may be said, are but petty malefactors, and not typical of a class. Ask wealthy natives of good position and honourable name if they are not themselves the victims of the petty assumption of the native official, and if something of the same sort does not occur in higher places, and directly under the influence of some whose characters are held up as deserving of respect by many of their sympathisers at home. One of these is a prominent leader of the extremists. He was formerly a member of the Indian provincial service, but forfeited his post on account of a falsification of registers, although a small compassionate allowance was made—and is still made—to him. So closely is he identified with the genuine native that, in addressing a recent meeting, he had to apologise for speaking in English, as the wicked influence of the *Feringhi* had deprived him of the power of speaking his own tongue with readiness. He is the proprietor of at least one newspaper, published in Bengal. Such papers would have little influence were it not believed that they are read and noted by the Government. If a well-to-do native gentleman neglects to subscribe, his attention is at first politely called to the omission. If the neglect continues, a tentative and non-committal article discusses the management of his estates. Sinister rumours are hinted at, which will be further dealt with. The subscription is then forthcoming, or the persecution continues. It is this intolerable incubus from which the loyal native is suffering; and it is this accursed blackmail on which some of the proprietors of the native Press are battening. The bitterest complaints I heard of came from native gentlemen themselves.

Undoubtedly, there is one underlying cause

of unrest in India which is independent of all politics, although political schemers may easily use it for their ends. The wisest observers know its operation, and no one spoke to me more decidedly about it, or recognised more fully the sinister political effect which it might have, than a gentleman of native birth, who is recognised universally as one of the leading citizens and most profound lawyers in Calcutta, and whose position and character command for him the highest respect. It is the economical difficulty, which is at this moment peculiarly acute in India, and especially in Bengal. This gentleman spoke to me of the deep-rooted, however ignorant, idea in the native mind—the inheritance of centuries of habit—that all social sufferings were to be ascribed either to the fault of the *Sirkar*, or Government, whatever for the time it might be, or to a curse resting upon that Government from heaven. By a series of uncontrollable circumstances, diverse reasons have combined to produce an economical crisis in India. The chief he considered to be the total failure of the hand-loom weaving, which was the principal industry of Bengal. The jute mills have only employed a handful of the millions who have lost their old industry, and even that employment has involved the abandonment of the country for the large towns. This vast social change has been accompanied by an enormous increase in the export of foodstuffs, and by a consequent rise in prices, that has struck at the poor with cruel severity. My friend fully admitted the stupendous difficulty of the subject, and the utter impossibility of a revival of the hand-loom industry. Whether an export duty on foodstuffs might become necessary was a question on which he refused to commit himself. But of this he was absolutely convinced—that unrest and agitation against our administration derived only a semblance of support from the side issues to which acute political agitators might appeal, and that its most real and most dangerous ally was one that came from the operation of economical laws, for which no Government could be held responsible, and which could be dealt with only by a fiscal scheme conceived on courageous and liberal lines, and unfettered by the maxims of any doctrinaire school of political economy.

To discuss this would lead me too far. I can only say that his horoscope of the political position seemed to me convincingly true. If we are to deal with it, we must begin by brushing aside the mischief-makers. As for Advisory Councils, local autonomy, schemes of decentralisation, and the rest—they may be right or wrong. They certainly command no universal adherence, and they seem to many to be playing on the surface, and to be something of the nature of fads. I heard some of the proceedings of the Decentralisation Commission. Within an hour and a half they ranged between a discussion as to the best form of village councils, the measure of social tact and conciliatory manners possessed by British officials, a discussion of educational administration—in which the members of the Commission seemed to me to be strangely unversed—and the relations between a powerful body like the Calcutta Port Commissioners and the Government. Does salvation for India, one wonders, lie that way?

XIX

COLOMBO

AT SEA: COLOMBO TO SUEZ,
January 12, 1908.

IT is worth returning from India by way of Ceylon, if only to see how strong is the contrast which Nature, in one of her humorous moods, has drawn between lands so close to one another. After we have crept slowly through the long, sullen stretches of the Hoogly, and have shaken off her slimy waters, we have four days of sweltering heat, with a following wind, no motion but a slow swell, and a fierce sun overhead. It is only as we once more get sight of land that rain-clouds seem to be gathering, and when we come within view of the Bassas Lights, on the east coast of Ceylon, the sky is heavy with them, and we have a foretaste of a new climate. Instead of the long, level plains of India, we have before us great masses of mountain, rising, in the far distance, some 8000 feet high. The shores are edged with yellow sands, and, just above these sands, dense groves of cocoa palms grow down to the sea, broken here and there by bright-coloured buildings, and, at the southern point, by the large port of Galle, with its towers and minarets standing out in vivid contrast with the deep green of the groves of palm-trees. In the early dawn the distant mountain peaks, some serrated and some rounded, rise clearly and sharply outlined; but as the sun comes up, dense clouds of white mist seem to rise from every valley and to embrace the hills in their folds, and soon the whole background is curtained behind a shadowy film of vapour. Whatever there is here, it certainly is not that drought which has burned itself into our memory in India, and which has parched up her boundless arid plains. We have still more than a day's voyage round the south coast of the island before we come in sight of the white lighthouse towers of Colombo, and are skirting past her long lines of sandy esplanade, and the red buildings that have a fine background in the palm groves that cluster round the city, and hide much of its extent within their leafy shades.

It is not Nature, but only the hand of man, that has made a harbour at Colombo. But artificial as it is, it is large enough to hold a goodly array of shipping, on its way to and from every quarter of the East. There are English, French, German, Japanese, and American ships—they meet here as at a sort of toll-bar, or crossing of many roads from East and West, and all have something to discharge and something to carry away from this common emporium. Colombo basks in a sort of luxurious ease on the harvest that she draws from the endless succession of vessels that must use her port.

You land at a convenient jetty, and on first stepping out from its sheltered arcade you might, so far as buildings are concerned, be in Portsmouth or Southampton. A tramway runs past; big shipping offices and public buildings, of red stone, crowd round in goodly array; a busy street of shops and warehouses leads up into the town. The delusion that you are in a European town does not last long; but Oriental as is the scene, its contrast, either with Bombay or with Calcutta, is sharp enough. There is none of the quaint and picturesque variety of the first, or of the life and bustle of the second. Except in colour, the faces you meet here are far different from all the Indian types, but they show little variety amongst themselves. The costumes are strange to us, but they are singularly and monotonously uniform. At first you can hardly distinguish men from women. All carry umbrellas; the labourers have peaked straw hats, such as you never see in India; and the men, with their smooth, weak faces, their hair twisted into bunches behind, and held by tortoise-shell combs (which are not dispensed with even when there is no hair to be confined within their circle), and their long skirts, look odiously effeminate. The ground is damp and slippery with rain, which we have ceased in India to count as a possibility of life. As we go farther, the buildings are less crowded, and the streets are bordered with thick foliage and broken by big compounds, where the bungalows are buried in a jungle of palm-trees and brilliant flowering plants, and where the shops are low booths, sheltering themselves picturesquely under the edge of the dense forest. We have the ox-wagons trailing along as in India, but here they are topped by a thick round canopy of straw, and they are varied by wagonettes and gigs, heavily hooded, and drawn by fast-trotting oxen, of a type quite unlike anything you see in India. Above all, the rickshaw predominates. At Durban one sees many of them—drawn there also by Eastern coolies. A few have penetrated even as far as Johannesburg. But at Colombo they are not the exception, but the rule. They flit past in an endless procession along every street; and at the clubs, the tennis courts, the hotels, and the big business premises—everywhere that the world of Colombo gathers—you find a crowd of waiting rickshaws, with their bare-legged attendant coolies. It is the dominant feature of the Colombo streets, and there are many means of travelling less comfortable and less expeditious than a well-drawn and well-appointed rickshaw with rubber-tyred wheels.

At Colombo no one walks, and you have to try the climate only for a very little time to know the reason why. This damp, enervating air reminds one of nothing so much as the steamy atmosphere of a forcing house. The pale faces of the white inhabitants, and, above all, the pitiful limpness of the few children that one sees about, tell their own tale. There is something peculiarly uncomfortable in watching the European nursery groups, perched in the ox-drawn wagonette, or making believe to play under the palm-trees, attended by an ayah in a low-cut evening dress, or by a male nurse with his flapping skirt and his back-knot and comb. Life in Ceylon is costly if it requires European children to be here. But, be it unhealthy or not, Colombo can boast a marvellous beauty of its own. At first sight it would seem as if it ought not to be without health-giving elements. Its splendid esplanade on the Galle Face, stretching along the coast eastwards, is swept by the sea-breeze, and would make the fortune of an English watering-place. It has abundance of open spaces, and indeed in some respects it is not so much a city surrounded by the country as a thickly planted garden, hiding in its recesses a great city of some 150,000 inhabitants. You may drive in any direction away from the business part of the town—"The Fort" as it is always called—and almost at once you are in roads surrounded by rich vegetation—now between tall hedges with copious blossoms like huge roses of yellow and pink, and now under the dense shade of the palm-trees or the delicate foliage of the flamboyant tree—a sort of flowering acacia—and the soft, feather-like branches of the beef-tree. In its temperature, in its damp and clammy heat, in its sub-tropical vegetation, in the promise—a somewhat deceptive promise—of the salubriousness of its sea-breezes, Colombo is more like Durban than any town that I have seen; but, rich as are the foliage and flowers of Durban, they cannot vie with those of Colombo, and even in the Berea of Durban I saw no gardens equal to those in which the bungalows of Colombo nestle below their canopy of palms.

Life has an air of exhausted luxury at Colombo which it bears nowhere in India. It is a perfect picture of tropical beauty, but we have an uneasy impression that it is a picture and nothing more. There is here no trouble of unrest to be dealt with. Political ambitions are not likely to be rife amongst these smooth-faced and effeminate natives. If they nurse ambitions, they must, one fancies, be chiefly of the commercial kind, which are already amply satisfied by stores of wealth, and which are nurtured on something else than threats of mutiny and vapourings of defiance. They find easier and more peaceable instruments in the quiet wiles and the subtle cunning that speak through these smooth faces and these shifting eyes. We have here no slumbering feuds of contending races to keep in check. There is no famine creeping in from time to time with relentless step, to be fought by patient and far-seeing effort. Even the plague, with its ill-omened allies in native usages and native superstitions, has not planted itself in Ceylon. This sleek, prosperous, smooth-tongued, oily race will never starve, and it will never fight. There are none of the gaunt spectres here that stalk through India; none of the fierce passions that are bred on her parched plains.

The ordinary civil servant here is not the strained and anxious warden of Empire that he is in India. He takes life more quietly, perhaps more listlessly, and he takes his pleasure with less of buoyant energy. He belongs to a smaller body, one, perhaps, more bound by petty conventions and traditions. As his ambitions are smaller, so his faculties, it may be, are less tense. One wonders whether, amongst the long catalogue of our dependencies, we have not rated too low our charge of this island, so marvellous in its beauty, in its wealth, in its vast opportunities. It is managed, not as a part of that great Eastern Empire which will furnish one of the most stupendous chapters in the history of our race, but as a section of a section of Colonial Office routine. Have not some of the parts of the machine which has, here in Ceylon, trundled along a fairly safe course of easy prosperity, become a little rusty and out of date? May not the culture of the Lotus have gone a little too far amongst the European and native officials, and may not the comparative ease of their task have made the sinews of the workers a little flaccid?

A breeze of healthy energy, more stimulating than any which blows from the sea upon the Galle Face, may come from the zeal and the administrative vigour of a new Proconsul. But he must have efficient instruments ready to his hand. It would be a fatal error if the routine of official tradition or tactless carelessness on the part of Downing Street were to stand in the way of the full development of this commercial Eldorado, and prevent the infusing of an energising impulse into every joint of the machine. In Ceylon we shall have no mutiny, and ambitions for self-government will never raise more than a passing and very ineffectual ferment. But the question still arises, whether weak hands have not, of recent years, been permitted to toy with the task, whether business-like efficiency has always been the first requirement, and whether vigour of administration has always been the tradition in Ceylon. Have we, in short, made, and are we making, the most of such a possession, on which covetous eyes may fix themselves, quick to observe any laxity in our hold of it, and will the hands of those who desire to brace the sinews of administration receive adequate support at home? In coming from India to Ceylon, one passes from the atmosphere of the strenuous arena to that of the Lotus garden. But the breath of a new energy is stirring; let us hope that it will not be discouraged or repressed.

THE END